Monologues
for Actors

of Color

Monologues for Actors of Color

Women

edited by Roberta Uno

Routledge
New York and London

Published in 2000 by
Routledge
29 West 35th Street
New York, NY 10001

Published in Great Britain by
Routledge
11 New Fetter Lane
London EC4P 4EE

Printed in the United States of America on acid-free paper.
Text design by Tara Klurman

Library of Congress Cataloging-in-Publication Data
Monologues for actors of color : women \ edited by Roberta Uno.
     p. cm.
   ISBN 0-87830-068-6.—ISBN 0-87830-069-4 (pbk.)
   1. Monologues. 2. Minorities—United States Drama. 3. Women Drama.
   4. American Drama—20th century. I. Uno, Roberta, 1956– .
PN2080.M536 2000   99-14171
808.82'45'082—dc21   CIP

For the many fine actors who have graced the stage
at **NEW WORLD THEATER**

Keep telling all of our stories

Contents

Preface viii

The Monologues

Big Butt Girls, Hard Headed Women Rhodessa Jones 1

Blues for Mr. Charlie James Baldwin 3

Breaking Glass Dmae Roberts 5

China Doll Elizabeth Wong 7

Cleveland Raining Sung Rno 11, 13

Cloud Tectonics José Rivera 15

Come Down Burning Kia Corthron 19

The Conversion of Ka'ahumanu Victoria Nalani Kneubuhl 23

Dark Cowgirls and Prairie Queens Linda Parris-Bailey 27

Diary of a Madwoman Chin Woon Ping 31

Do Lord Remember Me James de Jongh 35

Fish Head Soup Philip Kan Gotanda 39

Flyin' West Pearl Cleage 41

FOB David Henry Hwang 43

Foghorn Hanay Geiogamah 45

Funnyhouse of a Negro Adrienne Kennedy 47

Giving Up the Ghost Cherríe Moraga 51

The Have-Little Migdalia Cruz 55

Heroes and Saints Cherríe Moraga 59

How Else Am I Supposed to Know I'm Still Alive Evelina Fernandez 61, 63

The LA LA Awards Latins Anonymous 65

Latins Anonymous Latins Anonymous 69

Les Femmes Noires — Edgar White 73

The Lion and the Jewel — Wole Soyinka 77

A Little Something to Ease the Pain — René R. Alomá 79

Long Time Since Yesterday — P. J. Gibson 81

Miriam's Flowers — Migdalia Cruz 85

The Mojo and the Sayso — Aishah Rahman 87

My Ancestor's House — Bina Sharif 89

Night of the Assassins — José Triana 93

Paper Angels — Genny Lim 95

R.A.W. ('Cause I'm a Woman) — Diana Son 97

The Rez Sisters — Tomson Highway 101

Roosters — Milcha Sanchez-Scott 103

Sneaky — William S. Yellow Robe 105

Someday — Drew Hayden Taylor 107

A Song for a Nisei Fisherman — Philip Kan Gotanda 109

The Strength of Indian Women — Vera Manuel 111

Talking in Tongues — Winsome Pinnock 115, 117

Tea — Velina Hasu Houston 121

Unfinished Women Cry in No Man's Land
  While a Bird Dies in a Gilded Cage — Aisha Rahman 123, 127

Unmerciful Good Fortune — Edwin Sánchez 129

Weebjob — Diane Glancy 131

Wines in the Wilderness — Alice Childress 133

Acknowledgments — 135

Permissions and Play Sources — 136

Preface

While working on this and a companion collection for men, an incident occurred, poignant and revealing in nature, that spoke to the need for such an actor resource. The phone rang in the middle of the night and a young actor introduced himself asking, "Can you tell me where I can find a monologue written for a black, gay character?" Suppressing the impulse to ask him when my phone number had become an actor crisis hotline, I was intrigued by the desperation in his voice and the specificity of the question. When I questioned why he was looking for this monologue with such urgency that he had found it necessary to wake up a complete stranger, he apologized and explained that he was preparing for his final monologue assignment in four years of studying acting and, as a black gay actor, he had played a range of characters, but had never had the opportunity to inhabit the skin of a character who spoke to his most primary identities. He wondered aloud, did such material exist?

A symposium entitled "Training the Actor of Color," convened by the Tisch School of the Arts of New York University in 1994, brought this question to the foreground when actors of color in the audience spoke about their peripheral existence in major training programs. One observed that even in situations where the student is not an obvious racial minority in an acting class or a production, reading lists and course assignments typically draw from a very narrow and

Eurocentric canon. Another spoke enthusiastically about her experience acting in classics of European theater, but emphasized the special joy of speaking from the stage as a black woman, embodying an image often invisible or misrepresented in American society.

The issue of racial representation on the contemporary Western stage has historically been problematic, informed as it is by societal racism, a distorted and omnipresent media, the legacy of the American minstrel show, and the power dynamics of production. Although it's been some three decades since pioneers of the practice of nontraditional casting, such as C. Bernard Jackson, Joseph Papp, and Randall "Duk" Kim, opened the European canon to interpretation by actors of all races, surprisingly many theater directors still consider the idea new.

Ironically, for many actors of color, "nontraditional" casting would mean the opportunity to portray one's own racial identity on stage. Asian American actors are all too familiar with everyone from Marlon Brando to Katherine Hepburn to Jonathan Pryce portraying Asians; Native American actors suffer the "war-paint-and-wigs Indians" born of spaghetti westerns; and Latino actors see choice film roles consistently going to Anglo actors with household name recognition. All find themselves frequently cast as "backdrop" or "sidekick" to the story of a white protagonist in any number of settings—South Africa, Hawaii, Los Angeles, New York, the American West or South—where frequently they serve to teach that protagonist a profound lesson about humanity. Many actors share absurdly painful stories of being asked to audition "more black" or "more street" or with a thicker accent. In his unpublished solo performance piece, *Assimilation*, actor/writer Shushir Kurup portrays a South Asian actor following a casting director's instructions to become "more Indian"; the audience is mesmerized by his self-maiming transformation into a subhuman caricature that wins the unseen arbiter's approval.

This collection is intended to shift the point of focus from periphery to center, to characters who are more than setting for a "larger" story, the moral conscience of the story, or of tangential interest. My primary criteria were excellent writing, engaging acting material, and centrality of the character in the world of the play. I have chosen a range of contemporary excerpts, all from published sources, because it is essential that any actor understand the context of an isolated speech. Included are samplings of works that have clearly entered the canon, by authors such as Alice Childress, and Adrienne Kennedy, along with work by new, experimental, and international writers. Dramatic form includes traditional drama, as well as choreopoem, and text from solo performance, reflecting the aesthetic streams and impulses that have invigorated the contemporary theater.

A caveat: This resource is not intended to confine an actor within a box defined by gender, race, ethnicity, or national identity. I have seen, for example, white, Latina, and Asian actors interpret Aishah Rahman's *The Mojo and the Sayso* monologues with fascinating and different nuances and implications. What you have before you is powerful writing that promises to expand possibilities in performance and introduce a wider canon and an expanded, complex dramaturgy.

Roberta Uno
Amherst, Massachusetts

Big Butt Girls, Hard Headed Women
Rhodessa Jones

Big Butt Girls, Hard Headed Women "is a series of monologues based on the lives and times of real women who are incarcerated behind bars." It is "dedicated to the memory of Regina Brown, who was murdered in 1989 upon her third release from jail." The character Regina "is an African-American woman of about thirty. She is strong and aggressive and appears taller than she is." She was a "mother of two children . . . whore with a heart of gold . . . who, with a little direction, could have been running the world." In this monologue Regina lets the world know who she is.

REGINA: Fuck a bitch. Hit me! Bigger and better bitches than you have hit me. Just because I let you smell my pussy, don't make it your pussy. It's still my pussy. Everybody and anybody will use you so you best get to using first. I learned early, a man or a woman ain't nothing but a plaything. I tell them all, "It's like the lotto, baby. You got to be in it to win it." Later for all that "Ooh, baby" this and "Ooh baby" that. I believe in action, so you best get on with the A team. Like Tyrone, he's in love with me, always has been, and I can understand that. But I told him, "I was born a full-grown woman, and it ain't about 'my woman this' and 'my woman that.' I'm my own woman." But, like a lot of men, he don't want to listen. Wanted to

1

control me . . . thought he was my daddy. My daddy is dead, baby. And my mama raised me to be strong and on my own. He got all mad, 'cause he wasn't ready for the real deal. Brought some other girl, some Lily Lunchmeat-lookin' bitch I don't know, home! I told him, "Hey, if sister girl can hang, it's all in the family." Thought he was gonna work my nerves with that shit. And now who's crying? Tyrone. Because I'm carrying another man's baby. And that man ain't even important. The reality check has to do with me, my baby, and my baby's staying with Gerber's. I am a prostitute straight up. I decided a long time ago, wasn't no man gonna tell me what to do. I'm a full-grown woman, straight up and down. Or my name ain't Regina Brown. WORD! Hit me, bitch. . . .

Blues for Mr. Charlie
James Baldwin

Act 3. Plaguetown, USA. The court house. During the Civil Rights movement.

Lyle Britten, a white store owner, is on trial for the murder of Richard Henry. At the beginning of the play we see Lyle, a known racist, shoot Richard, the son of a respected black minister. Richard had returned home to the South after going north to seek a career as a singer. When he developed a drug habit, he came home to heal himself.

Juanita, a black student and leader in the civil rights movement, was Richard's girlfriend; the two met upon his return. Before taking the stand in court, she remembers her lover.

JUANITA: He lay beside me on that bed like a rock. As heavy as a rock—like he'd fallen—fallen from a high place—fallen so far and landed so heavy, he seemed almost to be sinking out of sight—with one knee pointing to heaven. My God. He covered me like that. He wasn't at all like I thought he was. He fell on—fell on me—like life and death. My God. His chest, his belly, the rising and the falling, the moans. How he clung, how he struggled—life and death! Life and death! Why did it all seem to me like tears? That he came to me, clung to me, plunged into me, sobbing, howling, bleeding, somewhere inside his chest, his belly, and it all came out, came pouring out, like tears! My God, the smell, the touch, the taste, the sound, of anguish! Richard! Why couldn't I have held you closer? Held you, held you, borne you, given you life again? Have made you be born again! Oh, Richard. The teeth that gleamed, oh! when you smiled, the spit flying when you cursed, the teeth stinging when you bit—your breath, your hands, your weight, my God, when you moved in me! Where shall I go now, what shall I do? Oh. Oh. Oh. Mama was frightened. Frightened because little Juanita brought her first real lover to this house. I suppose God does for Mama what Richard did for me. Juanita! I don't care! I don't care! Yes, I want a lover made of flesh and blood, of flesh and blood, like me, I don't want to be God's mother! He can *have* His icy, snow-white heaven! If He is somewhere around this fearful planet, if I ever see Him, I will spit in His face! In God's face! How *dare* He presume to judge a living soul! A living soul. Mama is afraid I'm pregnant. Mama is afraid of so much. I'm not afraid. I hope I'm pregnant. I *hope* I am! One more illegitimate black baby—that's right, you jive mothers! And I am going to raise my baby to be a man. A *man*, you dig? Oh, let me be pregnant, let me be pregnant, don't let it all be gone! A man. Juanita. A man. Oh, my God, there are no more. For me. Did this happen to Mama sometime? Did she have a man sometime who vanished like smoke? And left her to get through this world as best she could? Is that why she married my father? Did this happen to Mother Henry? Is this how we all get to be mothers—so soon? of helpless men—because all the other men perish? No. No. No. What is this world like? I will end up taking care of some man, some day. Help me do it with love. Pete. Meridian. Parnell. We have been the mothers for them all. It must be dreadful to be Parnell. There is no flesh he can touch. All of it is bloody. Incest everywhere. Ha-ha! You're going crazy, Juanita. Oh, Lord, don't let me go mad. Let me be pregnant! Let me be pregnant!

4

Breaking Glass
Dmae Roberts

Act 2. Scene 5. A dilapidated country house outside of Junction City, a small rural mill town in Oregon. 1977. A hot July.

Ricki is Asian American, the daughter of Mei Jen, a forty-two-year-old Chinese woman who is "beautiful, strong-willed, controlling." At twenty-two, Ricki "secretly writes poems while working at the same mill as her mother." She is "struggling to leave home and finish her last two years of college. Her mother keeps her at home with guilt and by convincing her that she can achieve her dreams if she works and saves money. She has difficulty in believing in herself or her dreams." Before his death, Ricki's father, Buddy, was a salesman, a Caucasian man who looked older than his forty-two years. He was overweight, smoked constantly, and was continually badgered by his wife, who regularly told him and Ricki that they were failures and lazy. He loved his wife deeply, despite her constant criticism.

Buddy died during a particularly ugly argument between Mei Jin and Ricki, which provoked his asthma and led to a heart attack. Although Ricki had previously decided to move out to escape her mother, she stayed and took over all of the funeral arrangements, cared for her mother, and attempted to understand her love for the father she never really knew and her complex and unhappy mother.

RICKI: Always writing. Writing. Always writing.
Her hands were tired from filling out forms. Useless
information. Then so many choices.
The color of the casket. How many flowers.
Leave his glasses on or not. Get
a reverend. How? He was a Baptist
who never went to church. She who'd never even
been to a funeral now took care of everything.
All. Everything in its place.

They said his heart stopped beating. Stopped because
he couldn't breathe anymore. Suffocated.
Now she sat under the canvas tent,
looking, looking at all the pretty flowers.
She knew the minister was doing the best he could,
not really knowing the family. Not knowing.
Then came her turn—her turn to speak. She glanced
at all the shadows also dressed in black.
She was ashamed she knew so few—the faces.
Friends he had, she never knew. His friends.

Words failed her though she tried to speak.
She wanted to say she knew him, that wasn't true.
After he died, she had to clean out his wallet.
She found two pictures inside—of her and her brother.
One as children—later together in high school.
Wanted to say she loved him, couldn't say it then.

And if he still lived. She couldn't say it yet.
Not to his face. His worried, heavy face.
She just couldn't. . . .

China Doll
Elizabeth Wong

A movie soundstage. 1940.

Anna Mae Wong, the exotic star of the silver screen, is now thirty-three. A "slender Chinese-American woman," she has been hired to teach a Caucasian ingenue how to play an "Oriental."

ANNA: Now, you see darling how it 'tis. My arms like so. My legs like so. Then, you have the suggestion of soft. The essence of femininity. And when your leading man sweeps you up and gathers you in his arms, you die a little. Like so. Just a small turn of the head. That's all. Isn't it simple? This is how they want to see a Chinese girl in the arms of a white man. You die a little each time. Now let's see you do it. (*She retrieves a Thermos, pours tea into a cup. A pained expression comes over her face, as the actress attempts an imitation.*)
No! No, no, no darling.
(ANNA *steps back into the light.*)
Well, it's interesting. But no. Look, this is how you look.
(*She takes an awkward pose.*)
We don't want that. No self-respecting Chinese girl thrusts out her breasts. And your neck! It's like a chicken at the chopping block.
(*She slowly corrects the position.*)

Bring your shoulders down. Your arms must be aloft. If you persist as you do, your yellow goop will rub off, your eye prostheses will stick to your leading man's nose, and the camera will see a white girl in bad makeup. Now let's try it again.

(*A pause. She watches.*)

Look, Miss Harrington. Sit down. Any chair. I know it's a difficult concept. Your New England soul can't fathom it. But remember darling, you are playing a Chinese. Therefore, you are a fantasy. You are sandalwood and jasmine. You are the promise of faraway places. But you are never real. You are not the mother. You are never the wife. You do not perspire. You are only a plaything—a China doll. (*Bitterly.*) China doll. Like me. But I never wanted to be a China doll. Pretty China doll. And now, my dear Miss Harrington, I'm teaching you how to be one. That is what they call ironic.

(*She puts up chair, sits.*)

(*Finds the page. Holds the script.*)

Now for your suicide scene. When it comes to dying, I'm the expert. I've died a thousand different movie deaths. You see an Oriental woman can fall in love with a white man, as long as she conveniently dies. Hardly realistic, nonetheless a widely accepted celluloid truth. Oh, we Orientals have so much to live up to. Anyway, as I read it, this scene of yours is fairly similar to one I played with George Raft, *Limehouse Blues*, 1934. We dance.

(*Á la Fred Astaire, she uses the ghostlight as a dance partner. Movie music swells.*)

Do you love me? Raft flings me to the floor. I crawl back to him. We dance. He's half Chinese. You are leaving me for a white woman? No, say it's not true. Raft flings me to the floor again. I crawl back to him. We dance. I love you. He flings me to the floor. I say to him: (*She clings onto the ghostlight.*) You are of the East. A white girl cannot bring happiness to you.

(*She moves away from the lightstand.*)

Then I betray him to the police. And then, I kill myself. I drink a strong poison. No, that's not it. I walk into the heaving dark and swirling waters of the Pacific. No . . . wait. I think that was *The Toll of the Sea*. Ah, I probably shot myself. Yes I think that's what it was. (*Pause.*)

What? Where were we? Sorry, shall we try your swooning technique? Scenes 17, 78, 102. Now swoon.

(*She watches impatiently.*)

Stop! What was that you think you're doing? That's not swooning. You do not buckle your knees forward and lunge like a buffalo. That is the American way of dropping dead. We Asiatics are much more delicate. Pay attention, please.

(*She gets up, demonstrates.*)

First the knees wobble, then you shift your weight to the right side, and then . . . the head falls back gently and slightly to the left. Then you press, not clutch, at his chest wherein lies his beating heart. Do you see the difference? Yah? Now you try.

(*She watches. Pause.*)

Nein, nein, nein. (*Pause.*) Absolutely, nyet! Think in oppositions. Oppositions! Try again. Swoon gracefully, please!

(*A knock is heard.*)

Yes, come in. I see. We're not through with the lesson yet, but I defer to duty. Miss Harrington, your limousine is here to take you to the location. Acting must come first. Well, we will continue our swooning tomorrow. Yes, same time. Goodbye.

(*Pause* ANNA *lights her cigarette. Another pause. She picks up the receiver of a telephone, dials the office of Samuel Goldwyn. Pause.*)

Hello? Mr. Goldwyn, please. This is Anna May Wong calling. Tell him it's urgent. It's regarding Miss Harrington.

(*A short pause.*)

Hello, Sam? Sam, I can't work with this girl. Sam, I can't take any more of this. I can't teach this starlet anything. Her swooning technique is atrocious. She's too stiff. She's slow. She's not right for the part at all. I showed her how to cross her legs, the way a Chinese girl would do it. Emphasize the silky line of your calves, I said. But she's a cow. Her eyes twitch like marbles in a sack. She's a nervous Nelly. She's no good. Sam, I can do this role. Let me have it.

(*A short pause.*)

Yes, yes. I know you need a scene coach first and foremost. Yes, but damn it, Mr. Goldwyn. This is killing me, Mr. Goldwyn. Please, don't discard me, don't put me on the shelf like a . . . China doll.

(*Pause.*)

Yes. I understand. We discuss this in your office. Tomorrow? The next day then. Very well. At your convenience. (*She hangs up the phone.*)

(*Long pause.*)

(*To audience.*) Why won't they let me do what I . . . what I love most of all? I'm not a teacher. I'm an actress.

(*Lights out.*)

Cleveland Raining
Sung Rno

Scenes 3 and 5. The Kim family house "in Ohio, about a hundred miles south of Cleveland. . . . An apocalyptic time."

Mari, a Korean American woman, is "a medical student in her early twenties. A healer." She lives with her older brother, Jimmy, a failed artist, who has been having visions of the end of the world by flooding. Mari is concerned about the disappearance of their father, who has been missing for nearly a week. The two siblings have been left on their own; their mother, a painter, abandoned them when Mari was a baby. Mari observes, "We're a family of leavers, aren't we? We leave Korea. Then we leave each other."

In this monologue, she has been sitting on the front porch reading a medical book. She closes the book and reads from her diary, reliving her dream.

MARI: This was my dream last night. I'm driving down the interstate and it's overcast. I can see the highway stretching over the plains for miles, but I look to my right and I see a farm, cows grazing, but past all of this I see trees stretched out across the sky, the stalks of wheat are like porridge like hair like someone's belly and then it seems like I can see even further, that past the fields, past the farms, I see . . . water . . . and waves and I can smell the salt the heat the taste of that sea.

I feel like turning the car into that wetness, that abyss. Only there's the shoulder, there's the guardrail, so I ignore it, I keep driving, I keep my eyes on the road. But I can't stop looking over there, into that invisible lake in the side of my vision, so finally . . . I do it . . . I turn I take a sharp turn I'm turning and—

Then I'm flipping . . . through the air . . . flying and flipping . . . over the barrier, up and over, there's the totally pure moment of silence, and then it's all noise: concrete, glass, the car the air the metal breaking, all of it breaking, and I'm bleeding, I'm in pain, I'm hurt, but I can't tell you, I can't tell you how happy I feel.

Cleveland Raining
Sung Rno

Scenes 3 and 5. The Kim family house "in Ohio, about a hundred miles south of Cleveland. . . . An apocalyptic time."

In the second monologue, Mari is again seated on the porch where there is now a makeshift bed made from a lawnchair. Storm, "a woman [who was] involved in a motorcycle accident," is recovering from her injuries. In her late twenties, she is also an Asian American woman; however, she rejects everything "Asian" and refuses to accept her own identity. In her diary, Mari remembers her infancy and the day her mother left; she writes of her continued search for her missing father.

MARI: (*Reading while writing.*) Someone's sticking their face into the crib. I'm sleeping. I feel someone's lips. Soft. Warm. There's that smell that I remember but I don't know from where. I open my eyes, my baby eyes, and I see my brother's face. He looks sad, he looks scared. Why are you scared, *Oppah*? Someone's shouting in the other room. Someone's crying. I'm crying. (*Stops writing.*) If that someone is me, then who is the other someone? (*To* STORM.) Can you tell me? A simple sign would do. I've been driving for over a week now. Still no sign of him. Driving so much my callouses have callouses. I dream in interstate miles, in state highways that bump and jerk through my head while I try to sleep. And still no sign.

13

Memory is my only weapon, my only hope. My friends tell me to move on, to leave this place. They don't understand. Escape doesn't always solve things. You can't just leave the pieces behind and expect everything to be fine. The past finds you. What you've done before, comes to your door today and tomorrow. Look at my mother and father. They leave their country, Korea; they come here, they make a better place. They think that they can just pick up where they left off. Just lift the needle off that record player, put another disc on, let the needle drop back down again. But see, the music has changed. You need different ears here. In this corn country, this state where flat is a color, and grey is a song.

Are you getting all of this? Because I see you Storm. You look like me. We have the same hair, the same eyes. Similar, not that different. Then I think I know you. I don't really, of course. But I think I do. And that gives me a strange kind of hope, a feeling that I can stay.

Cloud Tectonics
José Rivera

Echo Park, Los Angeles. "Aníbal's house, a modest pre–World War II wooden bungalow, working-class, not Hollywood."

Aníbal de la Luna, "a pleasant-looking man, thirties, dressed in an American Airlines ground crew uniform," encounters Celestina del Sol at a bus stop during a rain storm. She is "soaking wet. . . . It's impossible to tell her actual age. . . . She's very, very pregnant." When he takes her home, the digital clocks on all the appliances stop; throughout the evening Celestina experiences labor pains. Aníbal tries to ascertain who she is and she asks him, "what if there are people born who don't have that sense? Don't have that inner clock telling them when a moment has passed, when another has started. . . . I'm a fifty-four-year old woman, Aníbal, and I've been pregnant with this baby for two years . . . ."

In this monologue, Celestina gives Aníbal a synopsis of her life up until he found her hitchhiking by the side of the road, dropped off by a trucker.

CELESTINA: I think about sex all the time, though I've only had one lover in my life, only one time. Rodrigo Cruz. And I almost had two! That despicable trucker who kept touching my knees. But I ran away from him. I took my chances in the rain. But even he couldn't stop my endless daydreaming and nightdreaming about sex: about Rodrigo's ınkled back, my legs wrapped around his face . . . this obsession of mine . . . this tidal wave that started sometime when I was younger, when I lived in that one room. When Papi bought me a bicycle to give me something else to think about besides my body, and one glorious day I was allowed to ride around and around the house, because my Papi wanted me to count numbers, count numbers, over and over; he said it would teach me about the nature of "time," and I tried and tried, I really did, but I didn't learn anything, I was just so grateful to be outside my little room for once! (*Beat*)

Then Papi hired Rodrigo to work on his boat "The Celestina." And I would stare at him from my window as he worked. He was beautiful. I wondered if I was in love. And he would look back at me and stare and his hair was so long and black. And I wondered is that what love looks like? And I don't know how many years passed (I didn't know the word "years" then. I learned it on the road when the trucker taught me all kinds of words like "years" and "now" and "yesterday" and "minute" and "century") . . . and it must have been years . . . because years are longer than days (I learned this!) . . . and Rodrigo's hair was long and gray and he snuck into my room and did his dirty thing and left me . . . and my parents died in the other room and I went out to see because the house had grown so quiet and there they were in their little bed, holding hands, the green bedspread half covering their wrinkled bodies, they were naked and pale and covered in long gray hairs and very, very dead. That's the one time I stopped dreaming of sex when I called the police and told them Mami and Papi were dead, then I got dressed, and I lost all track of "time" and I got scared, and I ran out into the rain because I was sure they'd blame me and in my endless stay in my one room I didn't learn much, but I learned by reading detective novels that when somebody dies the police always come to take you away and kill you with a lightning chair. That's when I hit the road, pregnant, looking for Rodrigo Cruz, angry and excited because he was the only man I ever had sex with and I keep thinking about sex with Rodrigo and I love the word "sex" and if I could fuck fuck fuck all day I would!

Come Down Burning
Kia Corthron

Scene 4. Skoolie's house. In the mountains. On a hill.

Tee and her daughter, Evie, son, Will-Joe, and baby, Jazzman, are staying with Tee's sister, Skoolie. Skoolie "has legs that don't work. She gets around ably on a cart." She supports herself doing hair; she also performs at-home abortions. Jazzman won't suck milk from Tee and prefers to take a bottle from Skoolie. Tee and her family have been staying with Skoolie for free for four months: "I'm savin'. Get our own place. Me/Evie/Will-Joe/Jazzman place." Skoolie is doubtful that Tee will leave: "You ain't never stayed here less 'n six months at a time." She also suspects Tee is pregnant again. There are "two humps out back" where Tee's two infant daughters are buried, they were "Hungry. . . . Not enough for the last one and put a strain on the other three. Oldest two could take it. Youngest two couldn't."

Evie comes home with a bruise on her arm from her teacher. Tee goes to the school to complain about the mistreatment.

TEE: Appointment at eleven, bad for me, I miss mornin' work, good for Mrs. Shay, kids got the music teacher then, she free, so we do it. Meet at the secretary's office, I'm there ten 'til eleven. Wait. Wait, "Ten after, sure she comin'?" "She'll be here," secretary say, nice but fast. Wait. "Eleven thirty, she be here soon?" Secretary nod, secretary say "Eleven thirty!" call her over the loudspeaker, no answer. Quarter to twelve. Noon. I teary cuz I know music's over now. Secretary check her schedule. "She takin' 'em to lunch now," say she, "Catch her twelve thirty. She send the kids out for playground break, go back to solitude classroom half a hour." I outside Mrs. Shay door, five after noon, what she lock it for anyhow? I wait, belly growlin', smell cafeteria grill cheese, tomato soup, wait. Eight minutes to one she come, say, "Mrs. Edwards or Mrs. Beck?" cuz she know just two little black kids in fourth grade. I say Beck, she unlock door, I follow her in, she on and on "Evie a sweet little girl but limited attention span Kids watch too much unsupervise TV Parents always let 'em watch TV Won't tell 'em Read a book Won't tell 'em Do their homework Then come to school, no TV, they's bored." (*Pause*) . . . She got three piles. Papers, she pick up left sheet pick up middle sheet pick up right sheet one staple, clamp, upper left corner, make a fourth pile. She take next one next one next one clamp, fourth pile. Talk all the time clamp talkin' clamp clamp I stare at the stapler clamp She talkin' clamp She talkin' clamp clamp clamp clamp She talkin' clamp She not talkin'. Suddenly she quiet. Wait for me, say somethin'. . . . (*Pause.*) "Our TV been broke three years." . . . "Oh." . . . Then kids clamorin' in and . . . Evie come, Evie see me, run, grab me—Uh uh! Uh uh! "Don't tell her, Mama! Don't tell her, Mama, I fibbed! Don't tell her, I fibbed!" She tryin' to whisper, but too panicked, so loud enough Mrs. Shay can hear. Then Mrs. Shay tell her Sit down, take me out in the hall, shut the door and lean on it. She say . . . She say . . . "Somethin' a matter with Evie?" I say . . . "Well . . . " I say . . . "Well . . . got this big scratch on her arm." My head look down. Don't know what should say now. Hope she do. . . . (*Pause.*) Then she say . . . Then she say, "Somebody else at home?". . . I say, "Huh?" She say, "Evie's daddy or . . . somebody else? Come back to live with ya?". . . I say, "Uh uh! Jus' me, my sister.". . . I say, uh, I say, "Mrs. Shay, I gotta ask you how come that scratch on her arm." She look at me: I nuts. I say, "I think . . . I think maybe one time you pull her too hard." (*Pause*) . . . She say "Oh. I'm sorry." That all, she look at me, her eyes talk: "What else?" I say "That all, well, I guess that all.". . . I didn't cry! She never see me cry. She go back in the class, ten after one, I walkin' fast up and down up and down. Slower. Slow. I halt by the trashbasket sittin' in the hall. It full, I wanna pour it all out, fronta her door, but she gonna know I done it. I stoop by the trashbasket, by the door. If I wait 'til two she ain't gonna figure it's me I think, I think she gonna figure I left figure this done by someone else. So I stay stooped, still. But after 'bout ten minutes this little boy walks by, looks at me, wonderin'. I find the door says "Girls," go in a little stall, sit, my feet up won't no one know I'm here. Quiet 'til two, I wait ten extra, make sure. Tiptoe back, pour real easy, keep my face down case someone walk by. Only thing that make a noise is this stapler tumble out. Surprise. Perfeck condition this stapler and Miss Shay gonna toss it in the trashbasket. I grab it. I run. (*Pause*) . . . We need a stapler. . . . Skoolie. Never had one before.

The Conversion of Ka'ahumanu
Victoria Nalani Kneubuhl

Act 2. Scene 7. Hawai'i in the early 1900s.

Missionaries from New England have arrived in the Hawaiian Islands. Pali, a young Hawaiian woman in her twenties, is a favorite of Ka'ahumanu, the widow of Kamehameha. Her friend Hannah, a *hapa haole* (mixed Hawaiian/Caucasian) in her twenties, is immediately drawn to the Christian message. Pali resists Christian conversion, telling Hannah, "They're not good for us. They're teachings are false and evil." She scoffs at Hannah's assertion that ". . . we are all equal in God's sight." She retorts, "Then why aren't we equal on earth? . . . Things are different for you because you are hapa haole. They treat you so, bring you into their homes as a friend because they think you are half like them . . . ."

When it is discovered that Pali is a *Káua*, the daughter of outcasts who are marked and not allowed to live among the Hawaiians, she is badly beaten by the people in the village and rejected by Ka'ahumanu and even Hannah, despite her Christian principles. The missionaries treat Pali's wounds and offer her refuge from her persecutors. Because of their kindness and acceptance, it is Pali who wholly accepts their faith.

PALI: There was, when I was younger, a woman who came to live in the *hale* nearby who was with child. She was a strange woman, with

23

dark looks and knotted fingers. I knew she did not want her baby because many times I saw her gather plants to make a baby go away. But the baby wouldn't go away, and it grew inside her anyway. She had the baby in the dark, by herself, and when we went to see it, she told us to leave, that the baby was sick and would not live. (*Short pause*). One night, when there was no moon, I saw her steal out with the child all wrapped up. I followed her into the forest. She went far into the night and into the uplands where no one lives but the mountain spirits and the ghosts. I thought the baby had died, and she had come to bury it. I thought perhaps its sickness had made it unbearable to look at, and she wanted no one to see it, even in death. She stopped at a place that was quiet and hidden. I watched her put the white bundle in the ground. She began to walk very quickly back and forth, looking at the bundle. Then she would turn away and pull at her fingers. Over and over again she did this, until, finally, she turned and ran. Muttering under her breath, she ran away, and I watched her disappear like a thin ribbon into the night. And there in the forest I began to feel sorry for her. I felt sorry that she had lost her baby and could now see that she now suffered from terrible loss and grief. And I walked away from that place, looking through the black branches at the sky. I had gone some distance when I heard the first sound. It was like a small cry, so small I thought it was the far away cry of an owl. But it came again, louder, and a little louder, and louder, and I knew. She would leave her child while it still had life! The soft crying moved through me. I was sick. I ran back. I ran as fast as I could, toward the sound, but there was nothing there. I heard it again and ran, but nothing. And again and again I would hear and run, searching and searching, and find nothing. For what seemed like hours, I tried, but I could not find it again. Exhausted, I sat down and wept. I cried for everything: for the baby, for myself, my father, for all those like me in the world who had been cast aside and now suffered. I do not know how long I sat there so alone and abandoned and without hope. When all of a sudden it came to me, it was as if loving hands had laid a *kihei* on my shoulders. Comfort washed over me, and I was quiet. And in the quiet, I heard the voice, the voice of a baby, clear and strong, crying in the night. I stood and walked straight to it. I gathered up the small life I was meant to save. I had made a new life—not from my body, but from a thrown away life that no one wanted. I took the baby far away to a kind woman I knew would care for a child. I had given a new life. And now, that is what the *mikanele* have given to me, a new life from one that was unwanted, thrown away, and treated like so much rubbish.

Dark Cowgirls and Prairie Queens
Linda Parris-Bailey

Act 1. An evening camp gathering.

Dark Cowgirls and Prairie Queens, written by Linda Parris-Bailey and developed with and performed by her company, Carpetbag Theatre, tells the story of black women in the American West. This monologue is told by Black Mary of Montana, nearly six feet tall, a "fightin' woman." Mary "wuzn't shy with a weapon. . . . She'd tote a pistol and a shotgun too . . . [and] had a taste for big black cigars and hard liquor." During her long life, she worked a variety of jobs, starting as a nurse and moving on to hauling freight, driving a stage coach, running a restaurant, and opening her own laundry. In this story, she is close to eighty years old; she has just downed a shot of whiskey and grabbed a young "fella by his collar and knocked him down with her fist. . . ."

MARY: His laundry bill is paid. (*She downs another drink and goes to sit down . . . hears laughter*) What y'all laughin' at? You think 'cause Miss Mary is gittin' up in age she can't take care of her own business? You think I been runnin' a laundry all my life? You young folks don't know. Out here you either do or be done to, and I ain't never been one to be done to. Why I useta haul freight for a lot of folks. I'll tell you what made me give up hauling freight. It wuz a blizzard and a pack of hongry wolves. That's what did it. I wuz drivin' a team of hosses from Cascade to Fort Benton when snow started coming down like duck feathers on a slaughter farm. The trail started gettin' sluggish straight off slick too! Wheels wuz slippin' where they shoulda' been stickin' and stickin' where they shoulda' been slippin'. Hosses seemed like they wanted to pull in two different directions. I wuz drivin' as hard as I could, tryin' to get to Fort Benton befo' we froze to death on the trail. Almost wished I wuz back with those Ursaline Nuns.

(*Sits down and lights a cigar*) Woulda' been too if it hadn't been for that Bishop! Ol' Bishop fired me for a shoot-out I had with a fella. Unh unh, I like working for me. Wuzn't nobody tellin' me what to do. Heck wuzn't nobody tellin' me nothin' at all out there. Just me and them hosses on that trail. Least ways that's what I thought till I heard that long high howl come to me over the snow. The hosses started gettin' skittish, right off. Can't nothin' smell danger like a good hoss, I say. Well, they took to backin' up and goin' sideways, just pushin' each other from side to side. I held 'em just as hard as I knew how and I talked a blue streak to them animals, cuz they couldn't see in all that wind and snow. Whoa there boy, steady now steady. That's a good hoss, good hoss, easy now. Easy now . . . all of a sudden it got real quiet. Even the wind and the snow seemed to stop for a minute. It wuz so still that I stopped the hosses and I stood up in the wagon to listen. Somethin' told me to get ready to do battle. Just as I wuz reaching down to get my shotgun, a pack of wolves come up on the hosses just a snarlin' and barkin' and snappin'. Well, the hosses reared back, the wagon turned ovah, my shotgun went flyin' that way and I flew the other. (*Falls back in chair*) I musta hit my head on a rock when I fell—cuz when I woke up it was all quiet. My hosses wuz gone, my pistol wuz broke, and my whole load wuz dumped out on the prairie. I wuz having trouble feeling my hands and feet it wuz so cold. So I went ovah to the wagon and got some wood and dry matches and started me a fire. Just about time I started gettin' warm I heard that howling again. I went lookin' for my shotgun but it musta been covered by the snow. Then the wolves come up. I saw those beady eyes on the outer edge of the fire. Now I know I got trouble. I grabbed me a stick out of the fire and started wavin' it at those big gray dogs. They stood they ground, and I stood mine—no closer, no further away. Well, we stayed like that all night long. If I moved, they moved, and if they moved I moved. I guess we wuz tryin' to see who wuz gonna give up first. The sun finally come up the next mornin'. . . . Them wolves wuz sleep on the ground. I took what I could carry on my back, which wuz a considerable amount, off'a that wagon and headed for Fort Benton. I found a couple of them hosses 'bout twelve miles up the trail, so I didn't have to walk the whole way. When I finally made it to Fort Benton, I holed up there 'til spring. Warm weather come, I went back and got my wagon and quit. Some folks thought I shoulda give up hauling freight befo' that, but I liked the trail. Tried my hand at the restaurant business for a while, but I didn't cotton to feedin' folk. I missed the feel of being on the open prairie. The trail wuz freedom to me. So I took to driving a stage coach and hauling mail. Now that wuz a life. I won't tell you it wuzn't hard and cold too. I recollect drivin' up north sometimes and it'd be so cold my eyelids would 'most freeze shut. But I felt so free. (*Instrumental music begins—"Free"*) I didn't have to answer to nobody and I didn't depend on nobody neither. I ain't gonna tell you how I know, but I know what it feels like not to be free. Now I'm a big woman. I ain't scared of much. I ain't afraid of takin' no whippin'. I ain't afraid of givin' one neither. Why, I whipped some horses when I had to and I whipped some men too. I ain't a woman to take much off a' nobody. That's why I'll stay free.

Diary of a Madwoman
Chin Woon Ping

Act 1. Scene 5. Friday, May 13.

Madwoman is seen by her relatives as "an enigma . . . moody," and there is always something "vague or distracted about her." So they are quite surprised when she calls them all to her apartment after she has been "missing . . . for . . . two or three weeks." When they arrive and Madwoman doesn't appear, they break down her door to find out what happened. Seeing the mess that they expected, the elder relatives quickly settle down to play a game of mah-jongg while Niece and Nephew clean. The two curious youngsters find a diary in the microwave and begin to explore Madwoman's world.

Unraveling her story, they learn Madwoman is "a human being with dignity, and history, and integrity." Most of her writing is about a fear of being observed and recorded, "not wanting to be taped by men." She feels that electronic images and recordings will prevent her from being released "from all trappings and conveniences" limiting her desire to "soar like a dove above the roofs of managers and comptrollers and digital programmers." In this monologue she reflects on having been caught on camera at a convenience store.

MADWOMAN: (*To audience, miming the discomfort she feels, as if she* *were an insect or an animal under a microscope*) I was about to leave, but then I saw his eyes. First they were looking at me, looking me over, boring through me. Then, they looked away from me and up towards the ceiling! And that was when I saw the little camera pointed at me. He too wanted to tape me! And, from the way he looked at me and back at the camera, I knew he knew that I knew. It didn't matter what I did—all he wanted, all they all wanted, was to tape whatever I did, even if it was the most ordinary and harmless activity. I ran away as fast as I could (*With growing frenzied thrashing and discomfiture*), away from the shop, out of the noisy shopping complex, past the food court with all the fat people eating their fat meals, down the road crowded with so many suspicious characters and the noise of so many taping machines, up the stairs, and finally back to my room.

(*Spot on* MADWOMAN *standing in front of a mirror, with a lit candle. She sways the candle rhythmically, as if hypnotizing herself.*)

When I had calmed down, I started to think about what it was all these men wanted to tape of me. Yes, it didn't matter what I did, it was who I was. But who was I, that they had to tape me? What was I, *what* was it about me, that they wanted to *tape*?

When did men begin to tape us? I remember reading once that it had something to do with the building of the Great Wall . . . oh, old Qin was quite a conniver, he was . . . or, with Christopher Columbus . . . the massacre of the Pequods . . . the Amritsar troubles . . . something about conquering and controlling the other . . . *suttee*, dowry, footbinding . . . the Opium Wars perhaps . . . the conquerors thought women were contaminating and treasured *hyper*-masculinity . . . big muscles, big boots, big guns . . . ugh. (*Shudders*) Even today, men whose bosses snoop on them and insult them go home to kick their wives and steal off to tape their mistresses. . . .

I looked at my body, a little, puny, skinny, lonely thing. Is this what they wanted? Isn't it like anybody else's, like everybody's body? Is it because I have this (*Touching different parts of her body*) or this? (*Speaking as if in a hypnotic trance*) It's because they see who I am written all over my slippery little body. What they don't know is that sometimes the woman part of me just oozes away, until I am just a lizard mind, a bundle of nerves, a pack of cells, a network of urges and fears. No, they don't see that at all.

What they see is my skin—my iridiscent skin. What they want is to tape it and own it and do with it what they want, to sell their cars and hot dogs and be theirs to own. They want to turn me into something I will no longer recognize, to make me betray what I am, forget everything I believe in, so I will not even recognize myself anymore. Once they tape me they will know me and what they want is to know me thoroughly. There is a conspiracy to tape and tell, tape and sell. All they want is to secretly, surreptitiously, silently tape me and give the tape to the highest bidder. Wanting to tape me and each other, they look at each other with the deepest suspicion. . . .

I've got to let the world know. I've got to warn my sisters and cousins and friends . . . tell the whole world . . . they have to be warned about this conspiracy. . . .

Do Lord Remember Me
James de Jongh

Scene 5. The porch of The Old Folks Home for Colored in a Virginia Town. The 1930s.

Do Lord Remember Me was structured from verbatim texts, recorded in interviews of ex-slaves in the 1930s. "The lines and dialogue of this play are the words of Black men and women in their eighties and nineties as they recall their experience of the 'peculiar institution' as it happened to them nearly a lifetime ago. . . . It is an exploration of a collective memory, because some things should never be forgotten." The play is interwoven with traditional African American spirituals.

Henrietta King, an old woman with a terribly scarred face, begins the play seated in her rocking chair singing "A Balm in Gilead." The first character to speak to the audience, she says, "I ain't got no education and I don' know when I was born, but I do know I was born a slave, I'll tell you what I know and what I tell you is true, honey. . . ." At the play's end, Henrietta King tells us how she came to be disfigured.

HENRIETTA KING: See dis face? See dis mouf all twist over here so's I can't shet it? See dat eye? All raid, ain't it. Been dat way fo' eighty-some years now. Guess it gonna stay dat way till I die. Well, ole missus made dis face dis way. . . . Wanta know 'bout slaves days, do

35

you? Well, I'll tell you what slave days was like. . . . Marsa was a well meanin' man, but ole missus was a common dog. In de house ole missus was so stingy mean dat she didn't put enough on de table to feed a swaller. . . . Well, here's how it happened. She put a piece of candy on her washstan' one day. . . . (*Imagining the piece of candy to be resting on the block, becomes eight years old in voice and behavior.*) I was 'bout eight or nine years ole, an' it was my task to empty de slop ev'y mornin'. I seed de candy laying' dere an' I was hungry. Ain' had a father workin' in de fields like some of de chillun to bring me eats—had jes' little pieces of scrapback each mornin' throwed from de kitchen. I seed dat peppermint stick layin' dere an' I ain't dared go near it, cause I knew ole missus was just waiting for me to take it. . . . (*Crossing to the candy on the block, stuffing it into her mouth and sitting on the block trying to look innocent*) Den one mornin' I so hungry dat I cain't resist. I went straight in dere an' grab dat stick of candy and stuffed it in my mouf an' chew it down quick so ole Missus never fin' me wid it. . . . Next mornin' ole missus say, "Henrietta, you take dat piece o' candy out my room?" "No, ma'am, ain't seed no candy." "Chile you lyin' to me. You took dat candy." "Deed, Missus. I tell de truf. Ain't seed no candy." "You lyin' an' I'm gonna whup you. Come here." "Please Missus. Please don't whup me. I ain't seed no candy. I ain't took it.". . . Well she got her rawhide down from de nail by de fire place an' she grabbed me by de arm an' she turn me cross her knees whilst she set in de rocker so's she could hol' me. I twisted an' I turned til finally she called her daughter. De gal come an' she took dat strap like her mother tole her and commence to lay it on real hard whilst Missus holt me. I twisted way so dere warn't no chance o' her gettin' in no solid lick. Den ole Missus lif me by de legs an' she stuck my haid under de bottom of her rocker, an' she rock forward so's to hol' my head under de bottom of her rocker, an' she rock forward so's to hol' my head some mo'. I guess dey must have whupped me near 'bout an hour wid dat rocker leg a pressin' down on my haid. . . . Nex' thing I knew de ole Doctor was dere, an' I was lyin' on my pallet in de hall, an' he was pushin' an' diggin' at my face, but he couldn't do nothin' at all wid it. Seem like dat rocker pressin' on my young bones had crushed 'em all into soft pulp. De nex' day I couldn't open my mouf an' I feel it an' dey warn't no bones in de lef' side at all. An' my mouf kep' slippin' over to de right side an' I couldn't chaw nothin'—only drink milk. Well, ole Missus musta got kinda sorry, cause she gits doctor to come regular and pry at my mouf. He git it arterwhile so's it open an' I could move my lips, but it kep' movin' over to the right and I couldn't stop that. An' I ain't never growed no mo' teef on dat side. Ain't never been able to chaw nothin' good since. Don't even 'member what it is to chaw. Been eatin' liquid, stews an' soups ever since dat day, an' dat was eighty-six years ago. . . . Here, put your hand on my face. Right here on dis lef' cheek. Dat's what slavery days was like. It made me so I been goin' 'roun' lookin' like a false face all my life. What chilluns laugh at, and babies gits to cryin' when dey see me. Course I don't min' it no mo'. I been like dis so long now dat I don't never think on it, 'ceptin when I see someone starin' hard an' wonderin' what debbil got in an' made me born dis way. An' it was a debbil done it—a she debbil what's a burnin' an' twistin' in hell. . . . Used to see her sometime lookin' at me. Never did say nothin', just set there lookin' without knowin' I knew it. Guess she got tired of havin' me around. When I got thirteen years ole, she an' Marsa give me to Marsa's cousin. Was wid dem when Freedom come, an' dey let me stay on dere same as befo' 'ceptin' dey give me money each month. Stayed wid dem till I got married. Soon arter I got married, I heard dat ole Missus died. . . . Didn't make me drap no tears.

Fish Head Soup
Philip Kan Gotanda

Act 2. The Iwasaki house. A town in the San Joaquin Valley, California. Late
fall, 1989.

Dorothy Iwasaki is a Japanese American, a Nisei "in her middle fifties, but
still attractive, [a] waitress in a Japanese restaurant." At the play's beginning we see the Iwasaki family at the funeral of their son Mat, an event that
begins the disintegration of the family. In the next scene, Mat reappears,
returning home after several years following what we learn was a faked
drowning. An actor, desperate to make a film with an Asian American
focus, Mat has returned home to borrow money to finance the project. His
father is now an incoherent invalid, his brother, Victor, is a Vietnam veter-
an suffering from post-traumatic shock, and his mother is having an
affair. Returning home late at night after being with her lover, Dorothy is
confronted by Mat, "Who is this guy you go out dancing with till all hours
of the night? . . . The only . . . thing I see is you running around like some
goddamn seventeen year old in heat!" Stunned, Dorothy tells Mat about
the day he "died."

DOROTHY: I was standing there. The air was so still. I could hear the
voices of the workers calling to each other, they seemed so far away.
And I was so cold. The wet fog had seeped into my bones, so cold.
And I wanted to die. Not Mat. Not my son. Me. I wanted to take your

place. And I kept thinking if I could only make myself smaller and smaller it would be easier to die. And all the time I had this image in my head of myself holding you in my arms, a little baby, rocking you back and forth, back and forth. . . . I didn't have much—I wait on tables—but what I did have I gave to you. Not Victor, I gave to you. Because I could see the spark in your eyes, the Akari brightness, a willingness to live, not be afraid. I remember holding your hand and walking you through this house, you were five, six years old. And as we walked I handed you things. This vase, it was my ohi-ojiisan's, my great-grandfather's. I had you hold it, feel it. This kakeji, this scroll, has been in my family for generations. And this . . . I had you touch it, smell it, so you would remember, so you would always know who you were, where you came from. It wasn't much, but it was all I had to give and I offered it to you. To you. And what did you do? You threw it away. You killed yourself. You gave me a terrible gift, but I accepted it. I lived. I survived, to carry on the Akari name so these can be remembered, cherished. You can't stop me from feeling this. You can't make me die now. Not now. I am alive.

Flyin' West
Pearl Cleage

Act 2. Scene 4. A bedroom in a farmhouse on the outskirts of the all-black town of Nicodemus, Kansas. Fall of 1898.

Miss Leah is a black woman, seventy-three years old, who was born into slavery. She lives with Sophie Washington, also born into slavery, and Fannie Dove, born a free black; all three black women are homesteaders who have made a new family together on the Kansas prairie. Fannie's younger sister Minnie has returned home from London where she has been living with her husband, Frank, a very light-skinned black man, who was the illegitimate son of his master. Frank, "a colored poet," has been cut out of his father's will by his white half brothers. When Minnie refuses to sign over her share of the farm to him, he beats her savagely. Miss Leah observes, "A man that hit a woman once will hit her again." She comforts Minnie and tells her own story of violence and survival.

MISS LEAH: When they sold my first baby boy offa the place, I felt like I couldn't breathe for three days. After that, I could breathe a little better, but my breasts were so full of milk they'd soak the front of my dress. Overseer kept telling me he was gonna have to see if nigger milk was really chocolate like they said it was, so I had to stay away from him 'til my milk stopped runnin'. And one day I saw James and

41

I told him they had sold the baby, but he already knew it. He had twenty sold offa our place by that time. Never saw any of 'em.

When he told me that, I decided he was gonna at least lay eyes on at least one of his babies came through me. So next time they put us together, I told him that I was gonna be sure this time he got to see his chile before Colonel Harrison sold it. But I couldn't. Not that one or the one after or the one after the ones after that. James never saw their faces. Until we got free and had our five free babies. Then he couldn't look at 'em long enough. That was a man who loved his children. Hug 'em and kiss 'em and take 'em everywhere he go.

I think when he saw the fever take all five of them, one by one like that . . . racin' each other to heaven . . . it just broke him down. He'd waited so long to have his sons and now he was losing them all again. He was like a crazy man just before he died. So I buried him next to his children and I closed the door on that little piece of house we had and I started walkin' west. If I'd had wings, I'd a set out flyin' west. I needed to be some place big enough for all my sons and all my ghost grandbabies to roam around. Big enough for me to think about all that sweetness they had stole from me and James and just holler about it loud as I want to holler. . . .

[MINNIE: *I didn't want to sign it. I was just so scared. I didn't want him to hurt the baby. I can't make him . . . hitting me. I just . . . want him . . . to stop . . . hitting me.*]

MISS LEAH: They broke the chain, baby Sister. But we have to build it back. And build it back strong so the next time nobody can break it. Not from the outside and not from the inside. We can't let nobody take our babies. We've given up all the babies we can afford to lose. (*A beat*) Do you understand what I'm sayin' to you?

FOB
David Henry Hwang

Act 1. Scene 2. The back room of a small Chinese restaurant in Torrance, California, 1980.

Grace is a first-generation Chinese American college student. A young Chinese man encounters her in the back room of her family's restaurant and identifies himself as Gwan Gung, "God of Warriors, writers, and prostitutes." He has been wandering about Los Angeles, and Grace, although skeptical, is the first person he's met who knows who the Chinese mythological figure was. "Bullshit! . . . You don't look like Gwan Gung. Gwan Gung is a warrior. . . ." Intrigued by the stranger, Grace phones her cousin, Dale, a second-generation Chinese American, and invites him over; they decide to have dinner with her new friend, whom she introduces as "Steve." Dale's reaction to Steve is immediate and negative, "F-O-B. Fresh Off the Boat. . . . He's a pretty prime example, isn't he? All those foreign students—go swimming in their underwear and everything. . . ." As Dale and Steve engage in a painful competition eating food laden with hotsauce, Grace tells her own F.O.B. story about how she assimilated.

GRACE: Yeah. It's tough trying to live in Chinatown. But it's tough trying to live in Torrance, too. It's true. I don't like being alone. You know, when Mom could finally bring me to the U.S., I was already ten. But I never studied my English very hard in Taiwan, so I got moved back to the second grade. There were a few Chinese girls in the fourth grade, but they were American-born, so they wouldn't even talk to me. They'd just stay with themselves and compare how much clothes they all had, and make fun of the way we all talked. I figured I had a better chance of getting in with the white kids than with them, so in junior high I started bleaching my hair and hanging out at the beach—you know, Chinese hair looks pretty lousy when you bleach it. After a while, I knew what beach was gonna be good on any given day, and I could tell who was coming just by his van. But the American-born Chinese, it didn't matter to them. They just giggled and went to their own dances. Until my senior year in high school—that's how long it took for me to get over this whole thing. One night I took Dad's car and drove on Hollywood Boulevard, all the way from downtown to Beverly Hills, then back on Sunset. I was looking and listening—all the time with the window down, just so I'd feel like I was part of the city. And that Friday, it was—I guess—I said, "I'm lonely. And I don't like it. I don't like being alone." And that was all. As soon as I said it, I felt all of the breeze—it was really cool on my face—and I heard all of the radio—and the music sounded really good, you know? So I drove home.

Foghorn
Hanay Geiogamah

Scene #5. A Meadow.

Foghorn is a panorama of Native American experience which shifts between present reality and cleverly satirized moments in history. "Almost all the characters in this play are stereotypes pushed to the point of absurdity" portrayed "by playful mockery, rather than bitter denunciation." In this scene, the beautiful Princess Pocahantas has just returned from her first night with "the big, big captain." Surrounded by her eager handmaidens, she describes the tryst, with building suspense and pleasure in the tale.

POCAHONTAS: (*The Princess Pocahontas runs onstage carrying flowers and singing the "Indian Love Call." Her handmaidens follow, giggling. As Pocahontas flutters about, the handmaidens seat themselves in a semicircle for gossip.*) First, first he took me to his dwelling and he seemed, uh, kind of, of nervous about me being with him. He told one of the other captains that nobody was to . . . to come into the hut. This made me a little bit afraid at first, but he took hold of my hand and smiled at me. He kept smiling at me, and then he asked me, he asked me if I was a . . . a . . . vir-gin. When he said enough so that I knew what he was talking about, I . . . I said to him, "Yes, yes, I am a vir-gin." When I said this, he seemed to get

45

kind of nervous, excited. He looked at me deeply with his big blue eyes and told me that he was . . . in . . . in *luff* with me and he wanted me to . . . to . . . know his body and that he wanted to know, know my body too. Then he pulled me gently down on the bed and began to put his lips on mine. He did this several times, and each time his breathing became more, more nervous, like he was getting very warm. Then he began to kiss my neck and my cheeks. (*The handmaidens urge her on.*) And then he touched my breasts. And then he stood up, suddenly, and began to take off his clothes. He took off his boots, his shirt, his pants, all that he was wearing. He stood over me, his big, big, big body naked like one of the little children. There was so much hair on his body, it made me a little afraid. (*She giggles to herself.*) He said to me, I love you, dear Pocahontas. I promise you it won't happen the next time, I promise, I promise, I promise.

Funnyhouse of a Negro
Adrienne Kennedy

Act 1. Scene 5.

Funnyhouse of a Negro is a surrealistic play that explores the harrowing inner agony of a sensitive young black woman who cannot cope with the pressure of being black in America; her torment leads her through fevered dreams, madness, and suicide. Characters in the play represent aspects of her psyche and fragmented experience, a nightmare of memory and fantasy. Sarah, or Negro, appears first as a "faceless dark character with a hangman's rope about her neck and red blood on the part that would be her face. . . . On first glance she might be a younger person, but at a closer look the impression of an ancient character is given." She has "a head of frizzy hair," which she considers her "one defect," because it is "unmistakably Negro." The images of "wild kinky hair" falling out and baldness are repeated metaphors symbolizing self-destruction and self-hatred. In this monologue, Negro explains to the audience where she came from.

NEGRO: I always dreamed of a day when my mother would smile at me. My father—his mother wanted him to be Christ. From the beginning in the lamp of their dark room she said—I want you to be Jesus, to walk in Genesis and save the race. You must return to Africa, find revelation in the midst of golden savannas, nim and white frankopenny trees, white stallions roaming under a blue sky, you

47

must walk with a white dove and heal the race, heal the misery, take us off the cross. She stared at him anguished in the kerosene light . . . at dawn he watched her rise, kill a hen for him to eat at breakfast, then go to work down at the big house till dusk, till she died.

His father told him the race was no damn good. He hated his father and adores his mother. His mother didn't want him to marry my mother and sent a dead chicken to the wedding. I DON'T want you marrying that child, she wrote, she's not good enough for you, I want you to go to Africa. When they first married they lived in New York.

Then they went to Africa where my mother fell out of love with my father. She didn't want him to save the black race and spent her days combing her hair. She would not let him touch her in their wedding bed and called him black. He is black of skin with dark eyes and a great dark square brow. Then in Africa he started to drink and came home drunk one night and raped my mother. The child from the union is me. I clung to my mother. Long after she went to the asylum I wove long dreams of her beauty, her straight hair and fair skin and gray eyes, so identical to mine. How it anguished him. I turned from him, nailing him to the cross, he said, dragging him through grass and nailing him on a cross until he bled. He pleaded with me to help him find Genesis, search for Genesis in the minds of golden savannas, nim and white frankopenny trees, and white stallions roaming under a blue sky, help him search for the white dove; he wanted the black man to make a pure statement, he wanted the black man to rise from colonialism. But I sat in the room with my mother, sat by her bedside and helped her comb her straight black hair and wove long dreams of her beauty. She had long since begun to curse the place and spoke of herself trapped in blackness. She preferred the company of night owls. Only at night did she rise, walking in the garden among the trees with the owls. When I spoke to her she saw I was a black man's child and she preferred speaking to owls. Nights my father came from his school in the village struggling to embrace me. But I fled and hid under my mother's bed while she screamed of remorse. Her hair was falling badly and after a while we had to return to this country.

He tried to hang himself once. After my mother went to the asylum he had hallucinations, his mother threw a dead chicken at him, his father laughed and said the race was no damn good, my mother appeared in her nightgown screaming she had trapped herself in blackness. No white doves flew. He had left Africa and was again in New York. We lived in Harlem and no white doves flew. Sarah, Sarah, he would say to me, the soldiers are coming and a cross they are placing high on a tree and are dragging me through the grass and nailing me upon the cross. My blood is gushing. I wanted to live in Genesis in the midst of golden savannas, nim and white frankopenny trees, and white stallions roaming under a blue sky. I wanted to walk with a white dove. I wanted to be a Christian. Now I am Judas, I betrayed my mother. I sent your mother to the asylum. I created a yellow child who hates me. And he tried to hang himself in a Harlem hotel.

Giving Up the Ghost
Cherríe Moraga

Act 2. 1969.

Corky is "una chaparrita" who "acts tough, but has a wide open sincerity in her face which betrays the toughness." She dresses in the "cholo style" of her period (the 1960s): khakis with razor-sharp creases; pressed white undershirt; hair short and slicked back. She tells the story of being raped when she was twelve: "Taken me a long time to say that was exactly what happened. . . . But the truth is . . . I was took." A custodian working at the Catholic school she attended lured her into an empty classroom, ostensibly to help him fix a broken desk drawer. He asked her to stand holding the drawer while he used his screwdriver to tighten the screws. Torn between embarrassment, helping him, obeying him, aware that the screwdriver he held had become a weapon, she remained frozen in fear.

CORKY: *From then on all I see in my mind's eye . . .*
were my eyes shut?
is this screwdriver he's got in his sweaty palm
yellow glass handle
shiny metal
the kind my father useta use to fix things around the house
remembered how I'd help him

how he'd take me on his jobs with him
'n' I kept getting him confused in my mind this man 'n' his arm
with my father kept imagining him my father returned
come back
the arm was so soft but this other thing . . .
hielo hielo ice
I wanted to cry "papá papá" 'n' then I started crying for real
cuz I knew I musta done something real wrong to get myself
in this mess.

I figure he's gonna shove the damn thing up me
he's trying to get my chonas down 'n' I jus' keep saying
"por favor señor no please don'"
but I can hear my voice through my own ears
not from the inside out but the other way around
'n' I know I'm not fighting this one I know
I don' even sound convinced.

"¿Dónde 'stás papá?" I keep running through my mind
"¿dónde 'stás?"
'n' finally I imagine the man answering
"aquí estoy. soy tu papá."
'n' this gives me permission to go 'head
to not hafta fight.

By the time he gets my chonas down to my knees
I suddenly feel like I'm walking on air
like I been exposed to the air like I have no kneecaps
my thing kinda not attached to no body
flapping in the wind like a bird
a wounded bird.
I'm relieved when I hear the metal drop to the floor

only worry who will see me doing this?
get-this-over-with-get-this-over-with
'n' he does gracias a dios bringing his hand up
bringing me down to earth
linoleum floor cold
the smell of wax polish.

Y ya 'stoy lista for what long ago waited for me
there was no surprise
"open your legs" me dijo otra vez
'n' I do cuz I'm not useta fighting
what feels
like resignation

what feels
like the most natural thing in the world
to give in

'n' I open my legs wide wide open
for the angry animal that springs outta the opening
in his pants 'n' all I wanna do is have it over
so I can go back to being myself 'n' a kid again.

Then he hit me with it
into what was supposed to be a hole
that I remembered had to be cuz Norma had found it
once wet 'n' forbidden 'n' showed me too
how wide 'n' deep like a cueva
hers got when she wanted it to
only with me she said (pause)
"Only with you, Corky."

53

But with this one
there was no hole
he had to make it
'n' I saw myself down there like a face
with no opening
a face with no features
no eyes no nose no mouth
only little lines where they shoulda been
so I dint cry

I never cried as he shoved the thing
into what was supposed to be a mouth
with no teeth
with no hate
with no voice
only a hole. A Hole!
(gritando)
HE MADE ME A HOLE!

The Have-Little
Migdalia Cruz

Scene 14. The South Bronx. In the kitchen by the stove. Winter. 1976.

Lillian Rivera is a Puerto Rican girl, "innocent and spiritual." Fifteen years old, she has just had a baby and is living alone in the apartment she used to share with her mother. Her mother died six weeks earlier. Her father, an alcoholic, drops in and out of her life unpredictably. The baby's father died of a drug overdose before Lillian discovered she was going to have his baby; he was Lillian's first love: "I loved him so much. He never did nuffin' to hurt me. He was always my friend—it din't matter how dumb I was or how pretty. . . ." Her best friend, Michi, stopped talking to her after Lillian got pregnant. Michi and Lillian were very close, but Michi was determined to leave the neighborhood, chiding Lillian for not being more independant: "Don't you got a mind of your own? If I told you to jump off the roof, would you do it?"

At the time she got pregnant, Lillian stopped writing in her diary because "I'm no kid no more." Now, alone with her new baby, Joey, asleep in a cardboard box by the stove, she turns to her diary again.

LILLIAN: Dear Book: Hello again. You know what I did yesterday? Guess? Nah! Yep! I went to the store and asked the man for a newspaper and he give it to me for nuffin. He said I had big eyes people wif big eyes don't gotta pay for newspapers because . . . because they don't. Man, if I knew this before I wouldn'ta never not read 'em, you know. But alls I wanned was the cartoons to put 'em up on "Babyhair's" wall. That's my secret name for Joey. When I touch his hair it feel like a rainbow. He's one of those people, you know. The kind that got their sweetness on their heads. It's light. He's like a blonde. He almost looks like a movie star. Almost. (*Pause*) I always forgot what I was saying. (*Pause*) Oh. I put the cartoons up on his wall so he can learn how to read. But right now 'jus thinks it's a big toy he can't get at yet. I keep all his toys together in a big box, I got from the supermarket. It smells like vegetables, so all his toys smell like that too. . . . When I get hungry, I hold his teddy up to my nose. It's almost like eating. (*Pause*)

As soon as Babyhair's old enough, I'm gonna get a job running numbers and bring some money into this house. It's gonna be a fine house. (*Pause*) For just me and you, Joey. You're my only best friend now. (*Pause*)

I saw Michi on the street. I could've jumped on her and hugged her. She's been gone too long. She's not like me anymore. She's somebody else. Somebody that's going somewhere . . . and what am I? I've got three things that are mine—you, Don Quixote and the *Wizard of Oz* book I shared wif Michi. She should have won it. Mrs. Weiner just din't like her and liked me better. She should—she had me in seventh grade for two years. I just couldn't add anything up. I couldn't see two apples plus two apples and see four apples. I saw apple pies or birds picking at the apples or beautiful orchards filled wif apple trees, even though I din't know what an apple tree looks like. I mean, I seen them in books, but I've never touched one. I never grabbed an apple off a tree, right there, where it was created. I used to pretend I was this big, fat apple tree about to bloom. I thought this must be the way it feels, about to explode wif somefin beautiful. I wish I could see that place where things actually grow. (*Pause*) You're too quiet . . . babies shouldn't always be so quiet.

Heroes and Saints
Cherríe Moraga

Act 2. Scene 11. On the church steps. McLaughlin, California, a fictional town in the San Joaquin Valley. 1988.

Cerezita Valle "is a head of human dimension, but one who possesses such dignity of bearing and classical Indian beauty she can, at times, assume nearly religious proportions." She is positioned "on a rolling, tablelike platform . . . automated by a button she operates with her chin."

The agricultural town of McLaughlin is "a cancer cluster area, where a disproportionate number of children have been diagnosed with cancer in the last few years . . . as well as a high incidence of birth defects." The news media has arrived in the town because of a series of "crucifixions, performed in . . . a kind of ritualized protest" against the use of pesticides by the farm owners. Cerezita's mother keeps her hidden from public view, but Cerezita longs to be part of the world: "I want out . . . Out into that street!"

When a miracle occurs, the town's population streams to the steps of the church. Cerezita's mother brings her to face the procession of people who "bring forth pictures of their dead and deformed children in offering to la virgen." As the people sing and "pin milagros on the white cloth of her cart," she addresses the crowd.

CEREZITA: Put your hand inside my wound. Inside the valley of my wound, there is a people. A miracle people. In this pueblito where the valley people live, the river runs red with blood; but they are not afraid because they are used to the color red. It is the same color as the river that runs through their veins, the same color as the sun setting into the sierras, the same color of the pool of liquid they were born into. They remember this in order to understand why their fields, like the rags of the wounded, have soaked up the color and still bear no fruit. No lovely red fruit that el pueblo could point to and say yes, for this we bleed, for this our eyes go red with rage and sadness. They tell themselves red is as necessary as bread. They tell themselves this in a land where bread is a tortilla without maize, where the frijol cannot be cultivated. (*Pause*) But we, we live in a land of plenty. The fruits that pass through your fingers are too many to count—luscious red in their strawberry wonder, the deep purple of the grape inviting, the tomatoes perfectly shaped and translucent. And yet, you suffer at the same hands. (*Pause*) You are Guatemala, El Salvador. You are the Kuna y Tarahumara. You are the miracle people too, for like them the same blood runs through your veins. The same memory of a time when your deaths were cause for reverence and celebration, not shock and mourning. You are the miracle people because today, this day, that red memory will spill out from inside you and flood this valley con coraje. And you will be free. Free to name this land Madre. Madre Tierra. *Madre* Sagrada. Madre . . . Libertad. The radiant red mother . . . rising.

How Else Am I Supposed to Know I'm Still Alive
Evelina Fernandez

A kitchen in a house in East Los Angeles.

Nellie is "a 'well-endowed' woman in her fifties. She has bright red hair, bright red lips and bright red nails. She's wearing high heels and she's singing a song. She's carrying a grocery bag and a freshly cut rose" which she puts in a vase, smells, and smiles.

NELLIE: Well, Nellie, you still got it. Fifty years old and you still drive them crazy. So what if he was fat, bald and toothless. (*She laughs a big laugh.*) He's still got an . . . imagination (*She pricks her finger on a thorn on the rose.*) Ay chingado! (*She sucks her finger. Looks up to God.*) OK, OK. What happened to your sense of humor? I guess you think an old bag like me has no feelings anymore. Hey, I need my thrills too. You think cuz I'm old I don't need a little wink, a little smile, a little pinch on the butt? How else am I supposed to know I'm still alive. (*She goes to the sink and runs water on her finger and notices it's deeper than she thought. To God.*) Ya ni la friegas! (*She dries it off. The phone rings. She answers it.*) Hello? Oh, Hi Manny. (*She reaches for the grocery bag and takes out a pack of cigarettes and a package of store-bought tortillas.*) Of course I'm up. Are you? (*She laughs her big laugh, then catches herself and looks up.*) Just kidding. (*To* MANNY.) Of course I have coffee. (*She picks up the package of tortillas.*) And fresh homemade tortillas. (*She tosses them on the counter and lights cigarette.*) Yes, there are some of us that still make them by hand. Sure, come on over, I'll make you some breakfast. OK, Toodloo. (*She hangs up. To herself.*) Yes, Nellie, you still drive them crazy. And this one's not even a senior citizen yet. (*She pulls open the package of tortillas and puts them in a dishcloth then into a basket and into the oven. She turns it on, then opens the fridge.*) Let's see here. I think something simple but not ordinary. Something different. Something his wife never gives him. (*She laughs.*) We won't find that in the hielera will we. (*She looks up.*) Eh. You know I wouldn't do that with Manny . . . his stomach's too big. He'd have to be pretty enormous to get it past that pansota! (*She laughs, then stops.*) Hummm, maybe he is . . . Nah, his feet are too small. (*She starts pulling things out of the fridge.*) Aver . . . I can make him some huevos rancheros or . . . weenies con huevo. No, that was Louie's favorite breakfast . . . my Louie . . . (*To God.*) I don't understand you. A big strong happy guy like my Louie. Never sick a day in his life. He comes home. He sits down to eat. "I don't feel good Nellie. My chest I think I'm coming down with a cold." "Go lie down viejo, I'll rub some Vicks on you." And when I'm rubbing, thinking what a strong chest it is. Big and brown with muscles and hair, he starts choking. "Help me Nellie." Then, "I love you baby. . . . " Then he's gone. Just like that. You took him without even thinking about how much I needed that man; how much I was gonna miss him. Without even caring that I belonged to him and that without him I don't belong. You really piss me off you know that!

How Else Am I Supposed to Know I'm Still Alive
Evelina Fernandez

A kitchen in a house in East Los Angeles.

When Nellie's best friend Angie confides that she thinks she is pregnant after an affair, Nellie is overwhelmed momentarily with longing for babies she and her husband, Louie, never had. Angie coaxes her out of the bathroom, where Nellie has gone to cry. Apologizing, " I wish that God would've given you at least one. It's not fair that I had so many and you and Louie couldn't have any. . . .

NELLIE: (*Comes out of the bathroom. She smiles through her tears.*) But we sure had fun trying! (*She laughs her big laugh. She gets busy in the kitchen.*) And boy did we try. We'd make love in the morning, when he'd come home for lunch, and at night before we went to sleep. Boy, I loved that man. And he loved me. If he didn't he would've left me as soon as he found out I couldn't give him any babies. He wanted children so bad. We both did. We wanted them right away too. One right after the other. We wanted a house full of kids running in and out, yelling and screaming and fighting and laughing and crying. I pictured myself with one hanging onto my apron, one at my chichi and one on the way. So, as soon as we got married we got to work at making them. When it didn't happen at first we didn't really worry cuz we were having so much fun trying. Then a year went by. Then another. Then, we just stopped talking about it. After five years I remember I brought it up. I said "Viejo, maybe I can't have babies." He laughed and said "You never know honey, maybe I'm the one that's shooting blanks." It wasn't his Huevitos, it was mine. They weren't going where Louie's could get to them. Back then there wasn't anything to do about it. The day we found out we drove home from the doctor's and didn't say a word. Louie just held my hand and looked straight ahead. It was like we lost all the babies we never had. El travieso del Little Louie y La Preciosa del la Little Nellie and all the rest of them we'd dreamed of. I never cried about it. But Louie did. That night he cried like a baby. I held him and I sang to him until we both fell asleep. Then we never talked about it for a long time. Like we were in mourning. Till one day Louie came home from work in a real good mood. He sat down at the table and said "Come here, baby." I walked over to him. He hugged my waist, put his head on my panza and kissed it. "You know, Nellie," he said "God didn't give us babies cuz we love each other too much. How could I love anybody but you and how could you love anybody but me. But hey, that's O.K. with me. As long as I got you, Nellie, I'm a happy man. You're all I want. You're all I need."

The LA LA Awards
Latins Anonymous (Luisa Leschin, Armando Molina, Rick Nájera, Diane Rodríguez)

"Mary Qué"

The LA LA Awards is "a satirical, up-to-the-minute look at the Latino presence in Hollywood. All characters are broad versions of their obvious counterparts and should be played with ganas and love. Jokes and references should be updated whenever possible."

In addition to recognizing Latino celebrities like "Edward James Almost" and "Linda Roncha," achievement awards are presented to prominent figures not in the entertainment industry. In this scene, Edward James Almost introduces the business woman Mary Qué: "Enough about American me. I'm here to introduce a very important ruca who raised herself up from the barrio. . . . She's 'a toda madre-ruca-carnala-de-aquellas.' Look it up. A woman who combines bleach with brains. An Oil of Olay recipient. Let's give a great big Edward James Almost Orale to Miss Mary Qué, órale!"

MARY: (*Licking her lips.*) Mmm! Mr. "Stand and Deliver." Edward honey, sometime why don't you and I lay down and deliver. Ooo! Who would have thought that little ol' me from South Pico Rivera (*Or any local Latino community.*), born to a poor Mexican family, would have turned Mary Qué Cosmetics into a million-dollar empire for the facially handicapped. Oil of Ole! I can't believe I'm receiving a lifetime achievement award and I'm only twenty-five years old. It's unbelievable!

I personally want to thank the LA LA board members, whom I happen to have given personal makeovers to all night long. It was exhausting! Do you want to look like any of the stars you see here tonight or on "Siempre en Domingo?" Well, I can turn anyone into a cover girl or boy if you just use Mary Qué Cosmetics or become a Mary Qué distributor and win yourself a Pink Pinto. I started out small by making over my mother's side of the family. For example: (*Slide of a rugged looking "India"—Mexican-Indian woman.*) My aunt Malinche Guadalupe Gómez came in and needed help. She had just been through a messy divorce and needed a lift. So I said, "Tía, I'm calling you 'Michelle' 'cause your name's too hard for me to pronounce." She, like everyone on my mother's side of the family, had a flat face like a tortilla, dark illegal brown skin and a body like a tamale. I, of course, have worked on mine. So I did a little contouring and the results . . . (*Slide of Cher.*) Doesn't she look beautiful? Fifty years old! It's unbelievable! (*Slide of Guatemalan-Indian woman.*) Now my cousin came in and had a problem with her hair. (*Slide of woman with straight, stringy hair.*) It was straight and shiny. It had no body. Disgusting! I, of course, had hair like this and I knew exactly what to do. I processed it and gave her . . . (*Slide of horrifyingly plastic Loni Anderson.*) the "Loni Anderson Mall" look! She loves her new look and begs for more.

Now this woman came in, poor thing, horrible thick eyebrows and a moustache. Now, women, moustaches are not a problem. With my special technique it doesn't hurt a bit. I just pluck them out hair by hair and the results . . . I turned this woman . . . (*Slide of Frida Kahlo.*) into this woman . . . (*Slide of Madonna.*)

I care about selling you beauty, so your dreams will come true. American Dream—I can make it happen. (*Breathily singing, à la Marilyn Monroe.*) "Happy birthday, Mary Qué Cosmetics. Happy birthday to me. . . . "

Latins Anonymous
Latins Anonymous (Luisa Leschin, Armando Molina, Rick Nájera, Diane Rodríguez)

"Lolana Aerobics"

Latins Anonymous is a "comedic analysis of the contemporary Latino condition." Set in a meeting hall and parodying self-help and substance addiction programs, the characters begin their meeting with their self introductions: "Hi my name is _____. And I admit I'm a Latino/a." They share the "four H's to live by: We're not Hispanic. We're not Humble. We're not Hostile. We don't Hassle anyone about it. Damn it." This scene, written by Luisa Leschin, is her character's personal testimony.

To the sounds of driving rock music, Lolana crosses behind a scrim, doing jumping jacks, leg raises, etc. She is heard encouraging her class. "Three more! Feel the burn! Two more! Last one." She limps on stage, exhausted.

LOLANA: (*Calling off-stage.*) Good workout, girls! See you next week. Bye, Debbie, bye, Susie, bye, Buffy! (*To audience.*) Ay, those gringa workouts, they want to lose ten pounds in one hour! *Hola, chicas*! Welcome to Lolana aerobics! I'm Lolana and, ooh, I'm feeling good. Okay! (*She removes aerobic shoes and puts on spike heels in preparation for her class.*)

This is the Advanced Latin Woman's aerobics class where we exercise our femininity. And, *chicas*, don't let anybody kid you, femininity does not come natural, uh, uh, it takes technique! For today's class, our focus is going to be on . . . men! Oh, I like that! Okay! When you see a man you want, *chicas*, you've got to be like a heat-seeking missile. (*She picks a man and slinks over.*)

Hi. I know you're a man. Oh, I like that. Will you love Lolana? (*Pause.*) You see? Dead silence. Why? Because I'm using bad technique. You can't ask a man to love you, you've got to *inspire* him to love you. So, okay, *chicas*! Let's inspire! We're going to warm up our most lethal weapon . . . our hips! (*Shaking her hips like maracas.*) A Latina's hips know no rest. They work twenty-four hours a day. Dusting. (*Sings Santana's "Oye como va."*) Standing still. *Amorcito*, will you zip me up? When you're steamed! ¡*Coño*! (*Vigorously bounces from side to side with hand on hip.*)

See this backward and forward movement? Really good for when you're mad. Feeling mad!

Okay, *chicas*! Let's take a little breather. (*Wiping her brow with towel.*) Remember, we do not want to exercise too vigorously. If God had meant us to be skinny, he would have made us *gringas*! Let's do our first combination. For you busy career women, you can even do this in the office! First, you target a male. You! (*Walks over to the man and drops the towel all innocent.*) *Ay, se me cayó.*

Hips, remember, a good Latina has no sharp angles. Now you bend over and you pick it up. See what a nice fanny lift *you* get? See what a nice view you get. (*Indicating audience member.*) And for you, *chicas*, who prefer to work with cleavage, it's just a minor adjustment.

(*Turns around and shows as much bossom as possible.*) See? Ooh, feeling good. Okay, *chicas*, let's put it all together. This is very advanced, so don't strain yourselves. "Ay, se me cayó." (*Drops towel.*) No, honey. I'll pick it up. Ohh, you're such a strong man. (*In a deep plié.*) See how I'm looking up at the man? See how big and important it makes him feel? See how I'm toning up my thighs? Now, try to hold down there for as long as you possibly can. No pain, no gain! Three, two, one! *Ay*, okay, walk it out! Walk it out! Shake it out! Remember, being feminine means suffering, just a little bit.

This was a good workout, girls. Next week, we're going to make housework work for you. I'll teach you how to keep your man steaming hot while pumping iron. (*She pretends to iron.*) Feeling good! (*She dances off.*)

Les Femmes Noires
Edgar White

Scene 6. Mary Alice's apartment in the projects. New York. Evening.

This polyscenic play was "written from the viewpoint of a blind man perceiving sound." Taking place sometime between October and November in a New York City "spread grey across the canvas," the play focuses on black women workers who "restructure the architecture of the city as they enter the buildings of the dead, wrapped in new colours they go out and all men hope."

Mary Alice is about forty, crippled with a slight palsy of the legs. "Her affliction does not stop her life force. Her hands are very soft especially in the centre. She walks with a cane." Women are returning from work and gathering in Mary Alice's apartment. Carolyn, the twenty-three-year-old niece of a friend, has just been abandoned by her boyfriend. After listening to Carolyn's story of deception and betrayal, Mary Alice speaks of her own life and visions.

MARY ALICE: (*Alone*) This is the part of night I like best. Silence. So high up you don't hear the screams so much. So high up I didn't think a rat could reach up here, but it might. Early evening is prettier, after sunset. It's almost worth the rent here just to see that. But usually there is so much commotion here, you can't enjoy it. The time of day when the sky gets so dark and lumps of white cloud dissolve till you can't tell which is sky and which is cloud.

That gets me through the day while I'm in the office watching people kill each other quietly, and it's only because it's done so quiet that you realize you're not in the gutters. Everyday the desk that you work at gets older, and the longer you work at one place the better risk you are. So now you can get a loan which keeps you working there a little longer.

Every year somebody dies, they take up contributions, or they buy you a watch when you retire.

Sometimes when I'm coming home on the trains, I look to see if the conductor is a brother. I feel safer when it's a brother driving. I know he won't kill me because he don't want to die himself. When the train comes from underground at a Hundred-and-Twenty-Fifth Street, everybody is so shocked to see sunlight. They're not creatures for a minute, they have eyes like children and they stop breathing like beasts for a minute. When I dream I can always walk perfectly. I'm like a dancer then. My back is just as straight as Carolyn's. The muscles on my thighs love each other and knit themselves together just right.

Everything is so smooth in dreams, streets are marble like glass. No concrete anywhere to trip over, and the sunlight or the night stars always hit the walls of the temples just right. Just enough to make them jewels. (*Takes up glass again*) When I drink, it relaxes me. The nerve ends go to sleep, and my breathing slows down. (*Sits down flexing and unflexing her legs*)

Can't complain though, can't complain. I could be twenty and have niggers scheming how to use me, or I might have to live my life all over again days and nights. Like when my father said, "Girl, you black, you poor, and cripple. You can't even play no piano, you're just the last inkspot." He thought that was funny.

People just open their mouths and words come all out. You know, I'm beginning to think if nobody is watching, then no one is really kind.

(*Pause*)

You know.

The Lion and the Jewel
Wole Soyinka

Ilunjinle, a Yoruba Village. The Village Center. Night.

Baroka, "the Bale of Ilunjinle," sixty-two, has summoned his First Wife, Sadiku, and confided in her his real reason for seeking a new bride. He has recently found himself impotent and unable to perform even with his favorite wife: "I am withered and unsapped, the joy . . . Of ballad-mongers, the aged butt . . . Of youth's ribaldry. . . . I have told this to no one but you, Who are my eldest my most faithful wife. . . ."

In the next scene, we see Sadiku dancing derisively around "a carved figure of the Bale, naked and in full detail," mocking the chief's impotence and celebrating a female victory over the great Lion.

Sadiku: So we did for you too did we? We did for you in the end. Oh high and mighty lion, have we really scotched you? A—ya-ya-ya . . . we women undid you in the end. I was there when it happened to your father, the great Okiki. I did for him, I, the youngest and freshest of the wives. I killed him with my strength. I called him and he came at me, but no, for him, this was not like other times. I, Sadiku, was I not flame itself and he the flax on old women's spindles? I ate him up! Race of mighty lions, we always consume you, at our plea-

77

sure we spin you, at our whim we make you dance; like the foolish top you think the world revolves around you . . . fools! fools! . . . It is you who run giddy while we stand still and watch, and draw your frail thread from you, slowly, till nothing is left but a runty old stick. I scotched Okiki, Sadiku's unopened treasure-house demanded sacrifice, and Okiki came with his rusted key. Like a snake he came at me, like a rag he went back, a limp rag, smeared in shame. . . . (*Her ghoulish laugh repossesses her.*) Ah, take warning my masters, we'll scotch you in the end. . . . (*With a yell she leaps up, begins to dance round the tree, chanting.*)

Take warning, my masters

We'll scotch you in the end.

A Little Something to Ease the Pain
René R. Alomá

Act 1. Scene 3. A house in Cuba. 1979.

Cacha Rabel is the grandmother of two brothers who, after a long separa-
tion, are struggling to understand each other. One, Paye, is a playwright
returning to Cuba heavily influenced by his experiences in Canada; he wants
"to return to Cuba for good." The other, Tatín, says Cuba is a "mess. . . . My
radio show is being censored. My writing is being questioned . . . if I could,
I'd leave myself." Even though they are unable to fully grasp the other's
feelings or realities, they both respect Cacha and listen as she describes
the soul of their homeland, "the most beautiful land that human eyes ever
beheld." Cacha supports the government, her "youngest son died fighting
for Fidel." In this monologue, she relates a humorous incident of protest in
the days when Batista was in power.

CACHA: In those days, the beaches were not all public and there was
a section, fenced off so that Batista's military men could swim. A div-
ing board, a pavilion, lawn chairs and umbrellas. They had everything. The rest of us had to share two showers and a stretch of sand
no bigger than a sandbox. In the private part there were always
matrons looking like Eva Perón, covering their porcelain skin from
the sun. No negroes were allowed there. (*Laughs.*) But they say that

when a black man takes revenge, he does it with style. (*Giggles.*) You know what they used to do? They used to wait for the current to be flowing from the public section to the military and they'd swim over to the rope fence that divided even the water, and they'd shit and wave their load goodbye to the other side! (*Laughs.*) Once your grandfather was floating on his back out in the deep water, when the current suddenly reversed and all the turd kept coming back. He felt something bobbing by his feet; a shark?! No! It was a turd the size of a sausage. (*They're all laughing. The lights start to change slowly into a sunset effect.*) He never went to the beach again. That was in nineteen . . . forty-four. I haven't been to the beach since.

Long Time Since Yesterday
P. J. Gibson

Act 2. Scene 2. Ewing Township, New Jersey. Late summer.

When a group of black women gather following the suicide of their mutual friend, long-suppressed thoughts and feelings rise to the surface. Janeen Earl, the deceased, was "a follower" seen as "a little girl, innocent and naive" by her friends. Her childhood best friend, Laveer Swan, a painter, and Panzi Lew McVain, a physical therapist, have been at odds with each other since college. Laveer and Panzi were never able to share Janeen as a friend; now in their late thirties, their relationship continues to be fraught with jealousy and tension.

Laveer confronts Panzi with her knowledge that Panzi and Janeen had become lovers and that Janeen's husband, Walter, had discovered their affair. When Panzi is condemned by Laveer and the other women present, Panzi maintains that she loved Janeen. In her monologue she tells of her childhood suffering, the comfort she eventually found, and the healing she offered Janeen.

PANZI: No! I have the floor! My turn! . . . I was born the soul daughter to Adrelline Lucinda McVain. A very beautiful, shapely, silky-haired Adrelline Lucinda McVain. A woman known for her knowledge of beauty secrets . . . jewelry. (*Directs "jewelry" at* LAVEER.) A mother of three; two boys and one girl. A woman who loved men almost as much as her reflection in the mirror. She had to have her ego stroked continually, had to have euphoric adulation gracing her ears never-endingly. My mother, she had four husbands. All legal. Discarded them when they ran out of adjectives to describe her beauty. I used to wonder if she'd divorce me one day, discard me. I had nightmares of my brothers coming down to the breakfast table and finding my chair vacant and Momma explaining in her sweet, sultry voice, "Panzi didn't know how to talk to Momma. Momma don't share her roof with nobody who don't know how to talk to Momma." We'd heard that many times after Daddy disappeared, after Daddy Rudolph, Daddy Jimmy, Daddy Mason . . . My brothers, they learned early, caught on quickly, how to talk and stroke Momma. They'd hug her, kiss her, stroke her ego . . . and she'd repay you well for flattery. Buy you . . . presents. All you had to do was be a man and know how to compliment Momma. . . . (*To* ALISA.) And you talk of innocence. When my flat chest began to grow, Momma's eyes got colder, her words more bitter. There was no room for a girl child in my momma's house. When I was nine, I asked Momma for a Susie Walkmate Doll. It was the only thing I wanted for Christmas. I did everything just the way Momma liked them done to get that doll. (*Pause.*) Christmas Eve morning Momma got a phone call. I knew it was from a man because she took a long lavender perfume bath after she hung up the phone. She put on her makeup, her satin robe with the fuzzy feathers, her pink high-heel slippers. . . . I knew it was a man by the way her eyes bit into me. I hid when Mr. Jones rang the doorbell. I held my head low when he gave my brothers and me presents. I tried to disappear when he told Momma I was growing into a beautiful young lady. I prayed Mr. Jones hadn't messed things up. Christmas morning, no Susie Walkmate. Her excuse: the store had run out. . . . Momma never held me. On her dying bed in Mercy Hospital, she clutched my brothers' heads to her breasts, but never looked at me with those eyes. . . . (*To* LAVEER.) Your eyes. (*To* THELMA.) Where was your God and his laws then? Your God did not soothe me. A woman soothed me. She put her arms around me one cool winter evening while I was still young and she loved me, made me feel like I belonged in this world. A woman gave me that. (*To* LAVEER.) And Janeen, that Sunday morning, she needed these hands. . . . I understood her. I knew her longing. I'd been there. (*Fights tears.*) I didn't plan for things to . . . Why did you have to come back, stir up all the needs, desires, longings for . . . replicas? At first it was only friendship I needed, but the more you rejected, the more I wanted and . . . you became my sickness. Why couldn't you have just stayed? You had to conjure up all that wanting, needing, rejecting . . . Cut from the same cloth. That same beauty, same cutting edge. You and *Momma*. . . . Tell me, Laveer, what was wrong with me? *What was wrong with me?*

Miriam's Flowers
Migdalia Cruz

Scene 10. Delfina's apartment. The South Bronx. 1975.

Delfina Nieves is a thirty-six-year-old Puerto Rican woman whose seven-year-old son, Puli, was killed while chasing a baseball across the train tracks. His arm was never found; when he was buried, "They had to pin up his sleeve like a little cripple boy in his little box . . . small and white, like a little bathtub." Delfina, her lover and Puli's father, Nando, and her daughter, Miriam, are all struggling with the fact of Puli's death. Puli loved baseball and "always wanned to be in the paper like . . . Roberto Clemente." His death was published in the newspaper; they showed him, "How he was. All in pieces . . . the first one of us ever been in the paper. . . ." In this monologue, Delfina describes how Puli was dressed for his funeral.

DELFINA: He only wore his suit once before . . . to Pepe's wedding. I said it was stupid to buy a suit. Kids in suits look like midgets, especially boys. Or like monkeys. They always put monkeys in suits for T.V. shows. I didn't want my boy to dress like a monkey, but the bride wanted it like that—real formal. The shirt I had to borrow because the shirt he had didn't have no buttons and, you know, I couldn't find no buttons in the house to fix it, so a lady from the church gave me her son's old shirt, but it didn't even look old. It looked new. I think her son, Cholo, was always too fat for it. So Puli got it. The bow tie I got for him to wear on the first day of school. He wanted to wear a t-shirt, though, so he put his bow tie on the belt loop of his pants. He wore that almost all the time. When he fell asleep with all his clothes on, I could wake him up by unclipping that tie. He'd shoot up like an arrow, pull it out of my hands, and go back to sleep with that tie safe under his pillow. The socks are Miree's. All his socks had holes, and even though we had to fold them over twice, I think it's better, socks without holes. Especially since the shoes are new. He wanted those shoes for a long time—white, Converse All-Star hi-tops. Everybody said sneakers are disrespectful, but who was wearing them? Puli, and he knew what he wanted. I made Miree go to the church and ask for money. She hates me now. But Puli got his sneakers. They looked good on him, I bet. I . . . I couldn't look. Or maybe when I looked I just couldn't see. They did a good job on his face. They had to rebuild his head up again because mostly it—a good job is what everybody told me. Miree put a rose on top of him before they closed him up. That's supposed to be only for women, but you can't tell Miree what to do about nothing. I wish . . . I wish they had just showed his face. I didn't like seeing his arm like that, it gave Miree nightmares. She's not strong, like me. (*Fade out.*)

The Mojo and the Sayso
Aishah Rahman

Act 1. The living room of the Benjamins' home. Now. Sunday. Morning.

It's been three years since the death of ten-year-old Linus Benjamin, who was shot by the police in a case of mistaken identity. The check compensating his family for "Payment of Wrongful Death" has just arrived. Since Linus's death, his father, Acts, has submerged himself in building a car in the middle of the living room: "Soon I'll be finished [with] the dream car of my mind." Awilda, his wife, readies herself to go to church alone, as usual; still she urges him to accompany her to the special memorial service for their son. Acts responds, "We'll say no more about it. No more!" She accuses him: "You never talk about anything! Especially not about Linus! . . . LINUS IS NOT DEAD. I remember him. . . ." Picking up the compensation check, she wonders how her boy's life can possibly be measured in material terms.

AWILDA: (*Gingerly taking up check and looking at it*) UGH. I hate to touch it. It feels . . . funny. It's got an awful smell too. It must be the paper they use nowadays to print these things. "Payment for Wrongful Death." Big digits. Now we got lots of money. Lots of money for the life of our boy. How do they figger? How do they know? How do they add up what a ten-year-old boy's life is worth to his parents? Maybe they have a chart or something. Probably feed it into a computer. Bzzzz. "One scrawny brown working-class boy. Enter. No wealthy relatives. Size 4 shoe. A chance of becoming rich in his lifetime if he plays Lotto regularly." How many dollars? How many cents? Do they know about the time I found out I was pregnant with him? My absolute joy that God has sent me this child. True, I already had Walter but that was before you. But you loved us anyhow and soon Linus was growing inside of me because we were in love. Yes, there was never enough money and we were always struggling but that's just the way life is. We knew we were supposed to have this baby. You took me to your mother and father and sisters and all your sisters, brothers, aunts and uncles. Your whole tribe. You told them, "This is my woman and she's going to have our child." They all hugged and kissed me. Do they know about the way you would put your head on my stomach and listen? Did they figger in the way you held my hand with tears in your eyes when I was in labor? When he was born the grandparents, aunts, uncles, neighbors and friends brought presents, ate and drank and danced and sang. Do they know about those moments? Did they add them in here? And what about Linus himself? He would make me throw out all my mean, petty, selfish parts and give him the best person I could be. Remember when he was good? Remember when he was bad? The times he was like us yet someone brand-new? And . . . what . . . about . . . what . . . he . . . might . . . have . . . been? How do they figger? How do they know?

My Ancestor's House
Bina Sharif

Act 1. Scene 2. Rawalpindi, Pakistan. July 8, 1984.

Roona is a Pakistani woman in her thirties, married and mother of three children. Her sister, Bindia, has returned from New York City where she lives by choice, but is confused and unhappy. She was trained to be a doctor in Pakistan, but is unable to pass examinations to be licensed as a doctor in America. She has returned because their mother is dying and their youngest sister, Deedi, who has married badly, is very ill. Bindia dresses in jeans and smokes, in contrast to Roona's traditional clothing and lifestyle. Roona finds it hard to understand why Bindia chooses to live so far from their mother, yet she envies what she perceives to be Bindia's freedom as a woman in America. When Bindia confides that she feels "helpless, bewildered, alone," Roona shares her similar feelings.

Roona: I feel the same and I live right here in my own country. I work so hard to get my life going. I want . . . for my children . . . what we never had . . . and I have to bring up three daughters. In a few years, I will have to worry about their marriages and dowry . . . you beg or borrow. You have to give them jahez, dowry, expensive things. Otherwise, no man or no man's family will ever marry them, no matter how pretty, no matter how educated, if they cannot bring cars, frigidaire, VCRs, sofa sets, cutlery, jewelry, furniture with them as part of being brides . . . men in this country have never changed their attitude . . . they want more and more every day, their mothers want more and more every day, and if my daughters marry on their own—our society and religion will never forgive them like they never forgave Deedi. Even if I never care . . . even if I become liberated enough . . . society will never be liberated . . . then they will have to live with the guilt of choosing their own husbands and hurting us for the rest of their lives. And God forbid . . . if they choose the wrong men, like Deedi did, then we, the parents, will never forgive them. So I have to find husbands for them, I have to work hard to provide trousseaus for them. I work so hard. . . . I get up every morning at six o'clock, make breakfast for my husband, get children ready . . . take them to school, take the little girl to the babysitter's. Work in the office the whole day, with the men who treat us all like slaves— slaves, yes, now they call us "educated slaves." Then, I come home, cook dinner . . . by nine o'clock in the evening I am so exhausted I can hardly keep my eyes open, and my husband sits and watches TV and reads the newspapers. He thinks he is the last intellectual left in the world, and then he yells that one button on his shirt was missing and he felt embarrassed in the office because other men's wives sew the broken buttons on their husbands' shirts. He forgets that I bring three thousand rupees home every month, more than he makes. He forgets that, but he never forgets the broken button on his shirt. And still I cannot leave him. Where am I going to stand in this society if I leave him? A divorced or unmarried woman has still no place in this damn country. The men only seem modern, but they are modern for themselves. Not for us. There is no one I can com-municate with. I have no social life. I am an intelligent woman. I am struggling to find out why my spirit and my mind are failing. I had an absolute belief in myself . . . that was, and is, to some extent the only thing that keeps me going . . . I had belief in my father . . . and my brothers and my homeland, but I did not depend on them. I depended and trusted my belief in myself. That belief and trust I am losing. I feel as if I go down and down every day, there is a hollow, a space, a hole inside me which keeps getting bigger and bigger. I want to look around and find somebody—who can hold me tight and tell me not to be afraid. You are better off in America. Even if it is hard there. Bindia, trust me it is much harder here. And American society . . . must be so free, and different. So open. Just to be able to breathe. You could do anything you want. Be anything you want.

Night of the Assassins
José Triana

Act 2. A basement or an attic. The 1950s.

Cuca is a realist stuck in a room with her two siblings, who insist on playing a game that she considers "nonsense." They are "adults, but exhibit a
fading adolescent grace" like "figures in a ruined museum." The three
create roles for each other and explore the possible consequences of imag-
inary actions. "In this house, everything is a part of the game"; what's at
stake is "the salvation of your souls." The house is a "labyrinth" that "has
systematically obstructed all attempts to arrive at the truth."

Cuca's brother Lalo plays the part of an assassin and is tried by Cuca and
her sister for the attempted murder of their parents. In this monologue,
Cuca impersonates their mother, damning Lalo for his indiscretions. This
play has been seen by many as an allegory for prerevolutionary Cuban
society.

CUCA: (*as mother*). Don't you swear at me. You want to come across
as a fool, but I know your tricks, your games. I know them because
I gave birth to you. Nine months of dizziness, vomiting, aches, and
pains. And they were just the warnings of your arrival. Are you trying
to confuse me? Why are you swearing these things to me? Do you
think you've won over your audience? Do you think you can save

f? Well tell me, save yourself from what? (*Roars with laugh-* What planet are you living on, sonny? (*Mockingly.*) Oh, my little ︵ngel, I'm so sorry for you. You really are, well, I won't say what you are. . . . (*To* BEBA.) Do you know something, officer? One day he got it into his head that we should rearrange the whole house the way he wanted it. . . . As soon as I heard this ridiculous idea, I refused to listen to another word on the subject. His father hit the roof. You can't imagine what it looked like. . . . The ashtray on the chair. The vase lying on the floor. Awful! And then he started singing at the top of his voice, running all round the house: "The living room is not the living room. The living room is the kitchen." When that happened I pretended not to hear, as if I were listening to the rain. (*To* LALO.) You've only told the bits which interest you. Why don't you tell the rest of the story? (*Mockingly.*) You've told them about your martyr- dom, now tell them about ours, your father's and mine. Let me refresh your memory. (*To* BEBA, *transformed.*) Your Honour, if you knew the tears I have shed, the humiliation I have suffered, the hours of anguish, the sacrifices. . . . Just look at these hands . . . It makes me sick to look at them. (*On the verge of tears.*) My hands . . . If you had seen them before I got married. . . . Now I've lost every- thing: my youth, my happiness, all my little pleasures. I've sacrificed everything for this animal. (*To* LALO.) Aren't you ashamed? Do you still think you've done something heroic? (*Disgusted.*) You wretch. I don't know how I could have carried you for so long in my belly. I don't know why I didn't drown you at birth. (BEBA *bangs her gavel.*)

Paper Angels
Genny Lim

Scene 2. The women's dormitory of the Angel Island Immigration and
Detention Center, San Francisco Harbor, 1915.

Paper Angels is set during a time when racist immigration laws severely
restricted the movement of Chinese to the United States and prospective
immigrants were detained for long periods of time, months and even
years, on Angel Island in the San Francisco Harbor. Chin Moo is "an old village woman with a simple, practical outlook on life. At home in the Toisan
hill country, she is a fish out of water in American society. Yet she is
resilient and philosophical in response to life's demands." She has been
brought to America by her husband, Chin Gung, a Chinese sojourner to the
United States, "an old timer, with a taste for freedom and adventure."
When a younger woman complains about the five weeks she has spent
waiting, Chin Moo scoffs, "Pah! Five weeks! I have been on this Island for
three months." The young woman asks her incredulously, "How can you
stand it?" and Chin Moo tells her of the forty years she waited for her
sojourner husband.

CHIN MOO: When two persons are in love, they can live on water alone.
Everyone said we were heaven's match. I was never happier. He
taught me how to fish. We made baskets out of chicken wire with
openings on top. We'd put chicken hearts, fish heads, worms and

95

scraps inside and tie them to trees. Then we'd throw the traps into the river. By morning, we'd caught the plumpest, tastiest catfish, carp and crabs you'd ever sink your teeth in! (*Sighs.*) Then he got itchy feet. He had a burning desire to see the Beautiful Country. (*Sadly shrugs.*) So he left. He described everything he saw when he got there. But after awhile, the letters stopped coming. I let the incense grow cold in the burner, I left my hair uncombed. If you marry a dog, you must follow it. What could I do but sit at the doorstep and wait? . . . The women used to get together and gossip about *Gum San*. They told me the women there were bold and shameless. They ran around with flesh exposed like boiled chickens. Truly demons who bewitched men's souls by staring into their eyes. They made the men drunk so they'd spend all their money. They'd sleep with them, so they'd forget their China wives. Before long, the only names the men could remember were theirs. (*In disgust.*) Home? Forget about home! . . . When my mother-in-law died, I returned to my native village. I was ready to live out the rest of my days alone. (*Pauses.*) Then one day there was a knock on the door. Who could it be? I opened the door and there was my husband! Home after forty years! We both just stood there and stared at each other. I said, "Bick Hop," that was his name, "You have chicken skin and crane hair!" He replied, "You're no chickadee yourself!"

R.A.W. ('Cause I'm a Woman)
Diana Son

In *R.A.W. ('Cause I'm a Woman)*, four "Raunchy Asian Women," identified by numbers, speak as text appears on a projection surface onstage. Their comments, cynical, heartfelt, sarcastic, and passionate, are juxtaposed against pick-up lines, personal ads, and stereotypical phrases directed by men to Asian women. Finally, each woman steps forward with her own story, giving each a unique identity and voice.

1: Looking back I'm surprised we managed to love each other at all when the whole relationship was based on what we were not, who we were never going to be, what we weren't going to ask of each other. We were not a classic Korean couple. You did not pick me up from my mother's house in Queens in your top-of-the-line Hyundai. I did not kiss you on the cheek and tell you I had a nice time. In fact, we met in a dingy nightclub where you were dancing on the bar and I was shooting bourbon straight from the bottle. We took the subway to my apartment in Chelsea, fucked each other goodnight and I didn't have to tell you I had a nice time. I got involved with you *despite* the fact that you were a Korean man and I assumed that you made the same forgiveness of me. I grew to love your gentle wildness, your clumsy grace, your spirit your spirit. And I had leaned on the hope that there were similar things to love about me. I didn't want you to think of me as a Korean woman. Men who have been attracted to me for being Korean were interested in who I am only on the surface without knowing who I am in the deepest part of my heart. I am not ashamed of the presence of my heritage on my face but I mourn shamefully for the absence of Korea in my heart. You and I had an unspoken pact—I wouldn't be Korean to you if you weren't Korean to me. We went to movies, we threw parties, we spent many sweaty hours in bed and then one otherwise nameless night while my breath was still heavy and your legs were still pressed against mine you looked at me and said *sarang hae*. I had never heard it before. *Sarang hae*. You were telling me you loved me and I didn't understand what you were saying. *Sarang hae*. You asked me to say it. I couldn't say it. How could I use words that had no meaning to me to say what I knew in my heart. *Sarang hae*. The next time I say it I'll mean it.

5: A beautiful woman should never have to beg for the love of a man but I. Have begged because I. Am not beautiful outside no I know. They called me plateface when I was a child. Not just to tease me because I was Chinese because I was Japanese because I was KoreanThaiVietnamese all rolled up into one no I know. My face is flat and truly flat when I was a child. And company came we ate store bought desserts off of white china dishes. They measured seven inches across seven inches up and down and sneaking one into the bathroom I put one up to my face and seven inches all around it fit me. The plate fit my face like a glove. And my eyes are squinty. Small not almond shaped like the pretty geishas but slits like papercuts tiny. My hair is straight flat not shiny like the girl on the macadamia nut bottle but dry I got a perm it helps but I hate the smell. I have trouble finding men you're not surprised no I know. I took an ad out in the personal ads Single Asian Female looking for

Single Man of any race to love to care for to share bountiful joy with. Will answer all replies. I got a jillion replies a bouquet of hopeful suitors. I answered them all I said I would. It took days I found some nice ones. I arranged to meet them at convenient times in attractive places. The men came but they wore disappointed faces. I said I never promised you I was pretty. They said you said you were Asian—I assumed. I forgave them these men who were not so cute themselves. I held no grudge I let them off the hook. Outside I am ugly no I know. But I am beautiful in my heart yes God knows my heart is the home of great love. These men weren't beautiful inside or out. I missed nothing. I don't feel bad. This beautiful woman will never beg.

4: No one ever suspects me of being queer so its hard to score *dates* they're so *innocent* these women I mean get a *clue*. A hand on her thigh when we're sitting next to each other, a finger down her back as I stand behind her, a kiss on her neck instead of her cheek and they think "She's so warm." I'm so warm I'm *hot* somebody *notice* me Jesus *Christ*! What's a girl gotta do to get some attention from the same sex these days, stick my tongue down her throat and say "and I don't just mean that as friends"? I mean a good-looking girl should not have to spin her own bean as often as I do. And I know what it is I know what it is. No one thinks the nice little oriental girl likes to DIVE FOR TUNA. Likes to MUNCH MUFF. Likes to EAT HAIR PIE but I do I'm telling you I do. I've had plenty of guys as lovers and I can tell you that getting RAMMED that having someone's ROD IN MY FACE didn't really do it for me I like girls and as soon as I can get one TO LOOK AT ME like a woman I'll probably be . . . I don't know, maybe really happy. There was this woman at work, she wasn't even my type physically but she was really funny, I loved the way she used her hands the way she touched things. I wanted her hands to touch me I thought they would feel really good. So I flirted I asked her out I tried to kiss her she said wait. *Wait.* Are you saying you're gay? She was shocked she was embarrassed she said she had no idea. Why would a cute Asian girl have to be queer? I mean am I more cute than Asian? Am I more Asian than queer? And should I ask myself these questions if she wasn't willing to let me be all of them?

The Rez Sisters
Tomson Highway

Act 2. On the highway to Toronto from the Wasaychigan Hill Indian Reserve, Manitoulin Island, Ontario. Late summer, 1986.

"THE BIGGEST BINGO IN THE WORLD" is about to take place in Toronto, and the Rez sisters intend to be there. After a frenzy of collecting bottles, washing windows, picking blueberries, repairing roofs, baby-sitting, doing laundry, holding garage and bake sales, and working double shifts, the sisters are finally on the road. In the van, the women share intimate conversations during the long drive. Emily Dictionary, thirty-two, is "one tough lady": she wears "cowboy boots, tight blue jeans, a black leather jacket— all three items worn to the seams." A fierce fighter, she attributes her toughness to ten years of life with an abusive man: "Every second night for ten long ass-fuckin' years that goddamn Yellowknife drunk asshole Henry Dadzinanare come home to me so drunk his eyes was spittin' blood like Red Lucifer himself and he'd beat me purple. . . . " The night he came at her with an ax, she "grabbed one bag, took one last look at the kids and walked out of his life forever," taking up with a motorcycle gang, "Rose and the Rez Sisters." In this monologue, she tells her half-sister Marie-Adele why her motorcycle riding days are behind her.

EMILY: Fuckin' right. Me and the Rez Sisters, okay? Cruisin' down the coast highway one night. Hum of the engine between my thighs.

Rose. That's Rosabella Baez, leader of the pack. We were real close, me and her. She was always thinkin' real deep. And talkin' about bein' a woman. An Indian woman. And suicide. And alcohol and despair and how fuckin' hard it is to be an Indian in this country. (MARIE-ADELE *shushes her gently.*) No goddamn future for them, she'd say. And why, why, why? Always carryin' on like that. Chris'sakes. She was pretty heavy into the drugs. Guess we all were. We had a fight. Cruisin' down the coast highway that night. Rose in the middle. Me and Pussy Commanda off to the side. Big 18-wheeler come along real fast and me and Pussy Commanda get out of the way. But not Rose. She stayed in the middle. Went head-on into that truck like a fly splat against a windshield. I swear to this day I can still feel the spray of her blood against my neck. I drove on. Straight into daylight. Never looked back. Had enough gas money on me to take me far as Salt Lake City. Pawned my bike off and bought me a bus ticket back to Wasy. When I got to Chicago, that's when I got up the nerve to wash my lover's dried blood from off my neck. I loved that woman, Marie-Adele, I loved her like no man's ever loved a woman. But she's gone. I never wanna go back to San Francisco. No way, man.

Roosters
Milcha Sanchez-Scott

Act 1. Scene 2. The Southwest. The present.

Chata is "a fleshy woman of forty, who gives new meaning to the word blowzy. She has the lumpy face of a hard boozer. She walks with a slight limp. She wears a black kimono, on the back of which is embroidered in red a dragon and the words 'Korea, U.S.S. Perkins, 7th Fleet.' A cigarette hangs from her lips. She carries a bowl containing balls of tortilla dough." She is the irreverent sister of the legendary Gallo, a master cockfighter who has just been released from prison having served time for man slaughter. In this scene she addresses Juana, Gallo's long-suffering, faded wife, who is anxiously awaiting her husband's arrival.

Chata: Look at this. You call this a tortilla? Have some pride. Show him you're a woman.

(Juana: Chata, you've been here one day, and you already—)

Chata: Ah, you people don't know what it is to eat fresh handmade tortillas. My grandmother Hortensia, the one they used to call "La India Condenada". . . she would start making them at five o'clock in the morning. So the men would have something to eat when they went into the fields. Hijo! She was tough. . . . Use to break her own horses . . . and her own men. Every day at five o'clock she would wake me up. "Buenos pinchi dias," she would say. I was twelve or thirteen years old, still in braids. . . . "Press your hands into the dough," "Con fuerza," "Put your stamp on it." One day I woke up, tú sabes, con la sangre. "Ah! So you're a woman now. Got your own cycle like the moon. Soon you'll want a man, well this is what you do. When you see the one you want, you roll the tortilla on the inside of your thigh and then you give it to him nice and warm. Be sure you give it to him and nobody else." Well, I been rolling tortillas on my thighs, on my nalgas, and God only knows where else, but I've been giving my tortillas to the wrong men . . . and that's been the problem with my life. First there was Emilio. I gave him my first tortilla. Ay Mamacita, he use to say, these are delicious. Aye, he was handsome, a real lady-killer! After he did me the favor he didn't even have the cojones to stick around . . . took my TV set too. They're all shit. . . .

Sneaky
William S. Yellow Robe

Prologue. Late morning. Early 1950s. Outside a small stucco house.

Sneaky is the story of three Native American brothers who come together following the death of their mother and decide to give her a traditional burial. Descendants of a nomadic people, they traditionally buried their dead in trees, offering them to the sky. In the prologue we see one of the brothers, Frank Rose, at the age of ten or twelve. He is pleading with his grandmother, a woman in her sixties, to spare his puppy, who is to be slaughtered and given as part of a feast for Frank's recently deceased uncle. Grandmother explains why it "is the way of our people."

GRANDMOTHER: Don't bother me now grandson. (*She picks up the rope and prays with it, holding the rope in the air. She finishes and sets the rope down. She picks up the box and raises it in the air. The box wavers in the air. She steadies the box and prays again. After she finishes, she sets the box down. We hear a whimpering of a puppy from the box.*) Grandson, we eat puppy in honor of our people. Those who have died, or are receiving a new name or other honors. Those who have died and must continue on another journey are fed from our giving. (*Pause.*) There was a time when the people used the dog to carry their belongings for them. . . . And a time when we had a great winter and the people were starving. Because provisions promised by treaty from the government never arrived. And many of them died. A lot of them were your grandparents. (*Pause.*) In this winter, we could not bury the people in our old ways . . . our ways. And in the whiteman's burial we had to place them in the ground and cover them with dirt. We would be trapping their souls. This one winter, we didn't bury them in the ground like the whiteman wanted us to. The ground was too frozen and hard, thousands died one year. (*Pause.*) The next spring, one day, I was going to visit my cousins. I came by a little mound. I didn't know what it was, so I got closer to see. Then I saw this hole. It was a badger's hole. (*Pause.*) It was coming up and I wasn't sure at first, but he had something in his mouth. I looked real hard to see better. It was white whatever it was. As I got closer, I could see the mound was a huge grave. The badger held a hand in his mouth. When he seen me he charged me. Then he stopped and looked at me. In his eyes he was saying to me, "See. You didn't take care of this person. You should have taken care of this one." And then he turned and went back into his hole. (*Pause.*) We suffered a great loss. In time, the people had managed to feed themselves, their relations and even friends. They ate their dogs to live. Some of the people offered their dogs for a blessing of food. There was an answer from the Heavenly Father. . . . Before the steamboats came. . . . Long before the Black Robe Missions were serving their turkeys, cows and chickens.

Someday
Drew Hayden Taylor

Act 2. A fictional Ojibway community on the Otter Lake Reserve, somewhere in central Ontario. The house of Anne Wabung. The last week before
Christmas, 1991.

Anne Wabung is a fifty-three-year-old Native woman whose infant daughter, Grace, now renamed Janice, was taken away by the Children's Aid
Society and given to a white couple for adoption. Her dearest wish comes
true when her long-lost daughter, now a successful thirty-five-year-old
lawyer, locates her and comes "home" to meet her birth family. When she
presses Anne to reveal why she was put up for adoption—"obviously I was
taken away for some specific reason. Was it alcohol? . . . I am sick and
tired of the 'poor Indian' mentality. . . . Why did you give me up?"—Anne
explains that Grace was taken away.

ANNE: . . . "suitable." My home wasn't suitable. What the heck do
they know about what makes a home? I clothed you. I fed you. I
loved you. Out here that was suitable. When that investigator woman
stood there in my own kitchen not a foot from where you're sitting
right now, when she stood there and said I'd been abandoned and I
asked her what she was talking about anyways, and she said right
to my face that I was a woman whose husband walked right out on

her, I wanted to yell in her face, "Yes, I have a man and he didn't run out on me. He's a fine man gone to join the army to keep peace in this world and he sends me and his baby money." That's what I wanted to say to that . . . investigator woman from the Children's Aid. But I couldn't. Frank made me promise on the Bible not to, no matter what. He said it might get us in trouble. We got in trouble anyway. They took my little Grace right out of my arms and I never saw her again after that terrible day, God help me. They wouldn't even tell me where they took you. And poor Frank when he got back, and found out what happened, went drinking for four days. He'd never done that before. I almost lost it then but one of us had to be strong, so I was strong for the both of us.

A Song for a Nisei Fisherman
Philip Kan Gotanda

"Eating Fish" Scene 4. Stockton, California. 1974.

In a series of five scenes paralleling the act of fishing, *A Song for a Nisei Fisherman* follows the life of Itsuta Matsumoto through a cycle from childhood to death. Itsu is a Nisei, a second-generation Japanese American, who rises from humble origins to become a doctor. The different phases of fishing serve as a metaphor for different stages of Itsu's life, as well as a metaphor for the experience of his generation in America. This monologue occurs in his waning years; he reads the diary of his wife, Michiko, and learns of her repressed dreams.

MICHIKO: (*Enters, gradually overlapping.*) Sometimes I'm amazed I even stuck it out. (*Continues.*)
(FISHERMAN: [*Fading out.*] Sometimes I'm amazed I even stuck it out.)
MICHIKO: And don't think I wasn't tempted to leave at times. Remember when we first got married and how you used to stumble in from Mosan's poker games three, four o'clock in the morning and pass out dead drunk on the living room floor. I know, I know, "It's Mosan's fault, it's Mosan's fault." Who cares whose fault it was? I was the one who had to take off your clothes and somehow haul you into the bed.

And I was the one who had to clean up all the vomit when you threw up. Ahh, the romantic years. Some of those times I just wanted to pack up and go back to Mama and Papa, but I knew how much it would hurt them. Oh, things weren't always that bad and I admit I wasn't always the best wife. Remember the time I got so mad at you, 'cause you were always going fishing and leaving me with the kids and never helping out around the house, that I broke your best fishing pole. . . . I'm sorry. You know that's the only time you ever came close to hitting me.

(*Pause.*)

Twenty-eight years. I've been your wife for twenty-eight years. Cooked your meals, washed your clothes, bore your children. Right there by your side through all the rough times. You had things you wanted to do with your life, you had dreams. You cried when they seemed too far away and I comforted you. You yelled when you felt cheated from them and I took it all. And when you finally reached your dreams, I was so happy for you, though you never really thanked me.

I gave you two sons. They have things they want to do with their lives. Mommy do this, Mother do that. They have dreams. But what about my dreams, Itsu? What if, what if I could have anything I want? What if I could do anything I want? What would I want just for me?

The Strength of Indian Women
Vera Manuel

This play examines the policy of assimilating Native people "by removing children from the community and putting them in residential schools. . . . Beatings for speaking their own language, saying their own prayers or running away were often accompanied by the horror of emotional, physical and sexual abuse." In this play, "women tell their stories," opening "doors back to the future generations" and "unlocking the chains of the past."

Mariah, now an old woman, recalls a time when she was afraid to talk. Racially mixed, she remembers being taunted by whites and Indians: "my grandma who was Indian told me once, that it was not going to be easy livin' on the edge of two worlds." She savors the memories of living at her grandmother's house and remembers with grief her life after being taken away to boarding school. She recalls her schoolmates and the tragedies they experienced.

Mariah: I saw that girl, Theresa, refuse to stop speakin' Indian, refuse to quit prayin' to Napika (*the spirits*). . . . I saw her always encouragin' others not to forget they were Indian, and I admired her strength, and the depth of her determination. While no one else spoke to me . . . I had no friends, you see . . . she would always stop to give me a kind word, and I grew to love her like the older sister I never had. I'd sneak her extra food, she'd break it into bits and share it. I saw her challenge them again and again, daring them to do what they finally did to her . . . silence her. I saw Sister Luke—hate and venom spewing out of her mouth, "You dirty, savage Indian," she spat, and pushed that Theresa down, down two flights of cement steps, and I said nothin'. My screams were silent, and my agony and terror all consuming.

I saw murder done in that school, and when they wrapped that broken body and sent it home to the mother, tellin' her it was pneumonia that killed her little girl . . . she unwrapped it, and runnin' her grievin', lovin' mother's hands across the bruised face, shoulders, legs and back, discovered the neck was broken, screamed out in agony, "No . . . why? What has happened to my baby?" I said nothin'.

I saw little girls taken in the night from their beds. I heard the moans and groans and sobbing. "Shut up! Shut up!" I cried. Glazed eyes, ravaged and torn bodies returned in a frightened, huddled mass beneath the sheets, and . . . I said nothin'.

(MARIAH *feels the need to justify her inaction.*)

You're a good girl, they told me, these girls are bad, they need to be taught a lesson.

I saw a baby born one night to a mother who was little more than a child herself. I saw her frightened, dark eyes pleading with me to save her child . . . then later when the grave was dug, and the baby lowered into the ground . . . I said nothin'.

(MARIAH *turns her back, which is bent as though crushed by the weight of this story. Slowly, she begins to straighten her back and*

112

turning to face the audience, she explains her transformation, and visually we see her transformation as she purges herself.)

When my gran'ma died I was only nine, and I had no one. At Christmas and summer holidays, no one came to claim me, so "they" became my family. They stroked my light skin, and brushed my brown curls, and told me I was almost white. They pampered and spoiled me, and there was not a place in that school that I was not welcome. I had special privileges, and, because I was so good at sayin' nothin', I became one of them. I was very loyal. When I left that school, Father placed this gold cross around my neck, and he cried, and wished me well . . . made me promise to come back and visit. . . .

. . . I walked away . . . never looked back, not once. For a long time after that I couldn't pray, and for years I believed in nothin'.

Talking in Tongues
Winsome Pinnock

A flat in contemporary London. A party. New Year's Eve.

Completely dejected and alone in the midst of a party, Leela, a black woman, sits drinking and crying. Moments before, she discovered her boyfriend, a black man, having sex with the party's hostess, a white woman. Irma, "wearing a multicolored jumpsuit and trainers [sneakers], large gold earrings and . . . a bald head" has been "sitting on the floor in a corner cross-legged," observing Leela's state of misery. "As Leela sobs, [Irma] . . . laughs softly. As Leela's crying gets louder, she can't control her laughter and has to hold her stomach." Leela notices her and stops crying as Irma approaches. Irma "can be played by either a male or female performer." In their brief alcohol-tinged encounter, Irma alludes to a central theme of the play: finding expression for one's innermost emotions. She asks Leela, "Have you never felt the spirit stirring inside you?"

IRMA: You were crying. It always ends in tears. Either that or the china gets broken. (*Pause.*) You don't say much, do you? Not that it matters. I can talk the hind legs off an armchair. (*Pause.*) I was born in south London thirty years ago. My birth was the occasion of great trauma for my mother who, prior to going into labour, had witnessed the strange couplings of common or garden slugs on her kitchen floor at midnight. It wasn't the bizarreness of their copulation that struck her but the realisation that each partner had both projectile and receptacle—she was very fastidious—which, in effect, made the sex act redundant as a particularly flexible slug could impregnate itself. That such a phenomenon existed on God's earth—she was also very superstitious—undermined the very tenets by which she'd thus far kept her life together. She felt cheated. If God had seen fit to bestow this gift upon human beings then she would not have had to undergo the ritual Friday Night Fuck, a particularly vigorous, not to mention careless, session of which had resulted in my conception. She was overwhelmed by the depth of her anger, and the shock of it propelled her into labour. The doctors didn't know how to tell her at first. It doesn't happen very often, but sometimes a child is born with both receptacle and projectile nestling between its legs. I was such a child and the doctors told my mother that she had to make a choice, or I would be plagued by severe mental confusion and distress for the rest of my life. Of course she didn't know which way to turn. In the end she settled on getting rid of the male appendage, not least because she held the things in contempt but also because she felt that black men were too often in the limelight, and that a woman might quietly get things done while those who undermined her were looking the other way. However, she hadn't reckoned with the fact that she had already become attached to me and found me perfect the way I was. So even while the surgeon was sharpening his knives my mother had wrapped me in an old shawl, woven by her own grandmother, and taken me home. I hope I'm not boring you. . . .

Talking in Tongues
Winsome Pinnock

Prologue. A beach in Jamaica. A very bright day.

After Leela's relationship ends she goes on holiday in Jamaica with a woman friend. In the early morning she encounters Sugar, a Jamaican woman who was the unintended victim of a prank played by Leela and her friend. Sugar has lost her domestic job at the hotel and Irma feels guilty. When Sugar rejects her apology by saying, "What you want from me? . . . What happen to unno make you so broken?" Leela grows more and more emotional, "Broken, yes. Invisible people. . . . I hate the world that tries to stifle me . . . I'm angry with myself . . . I want revenge. I want to lash out. . . ." Her "speech becomes a garble as she struggles to get the words out, her body trembling out of her control. . . ." She starts to mutter incoherently until she "starts to talk in tongues." Sugar is "bewildered at first," then frightened at "all the rage and anger that Leela has repressed for so long." When the outburst subsides, Sugar holds the exhausted Leela and "rocks her from side to side like a baby," soothing her. This prologue to the play occurs in chronological time after this point. It is Sugar's memory of "a language that go back before race."

SUGAR: Them used to say them was going down a gully fe go wash clothes, but the way them women leave dragging themself like them have rock tie to them foot, then come back skipping like children

117

make everybody suspec' them have some business a gully that have nothing to do with dirty washing. Sometimes them man would try to follow back a dem, but they would only reach so far before something bad happen: one a them get lost in a bush, grow round him while he was walking; another man get bite up by a snake and haffe quick hop home and bind up him foot, an' a nex' one suck up inna hurricane lie dizzy ina bed for a week. No man ever find them.

There were three of them: Jo-Jo, a big, mighty woman who everybody used to say batter her husband; Dum-Dum, a woman who never speak; and Mary, a good, gentle woman who would give you her last penny even if she was starving. These women were a mystery to me. Every day them like every other woman, cooking and cleaning for them husband, except this one afternoon when them bundle up them clothes and go off by themself. I couldn't wait to grow up to discover the mystery of womanness for meself. I used to sit and stare at them to see if I could see it on them, but I couldn't. So one day I follow them. I was nine years old.

I wait for them to leave, pretending like I wasn't taking any notice a them, then after a few minutes I went after them. Me have to run hard to keep up with them. It look like they was walking slowly, them hip a swing from side to side under them frock, but they was moving further and further away from me, so I run as fast as my little leg would go and still they would be ahead of me. Then they come to a gully I never see before—a huge waterfall falling over great white rock. I hide meself behind a rockstone and watch.

Them take them clothes out a the basket and start to wash them in the water, slapping them against rock, then rub them under the water and slap them against rock, lie them out to dry in the sun.

Then they start again, slap clothes against rock, rinse them under running water and lie them out to dry. Slap, rinse, slap slap, rinse dry. Them never say anything to one another, never even look at one another, for musse half an hour or more.

I was so disappointed I could cry. I thought I was going to see a woman fly. I thought woman was a mystery—click her fingers and fire would fly out—but woman was just washing clothes. Woman was washing clothes then going home and cooking food for man. I had tears in my eyes. Me ready fe run till one a them start to hum. It seem like everything stop and listen to that humming, the breeze still, the water hush up. Then the other women join in, singing together like in one voice. You couldn't move when you hear them singing. Then them start to sway. Dum-Dum, the silent woman, was in the middle, she start to sway and rise up on her toes like there was something inside her, pulling her up. The other women start to sway too and rise up, and I tell you I see the spirit rise in them women. Them start to tremble and make little jump till they was jumping around like them didn't know where them was. Then all of a sudden the silent woman stand very still like her body seize up and lift her head to the sky and start to call out. She was shouting—a woman I never hear say a word in my life—was shouting to the sky loud loud and saying words very fast in a language you never hear before. A woman who couldn't even talk, filling the sky with words in a language must be not spoken in a million years, a language that go back before race. She lift her fist and strike out one more time. After, she collapse, but the other women catch her before she fall. She just lie there, like she sleeping, and the other women finish washing her clothes for her. When she wake up they give her something to drink and they all go home like nothing happen. I always wonder what madness them release when they shout out like that.

(*Slight pause.*) But all that finish now, them women dead off long time. Me, I just go walk down by the beach, lift weight, jog, take aerobic exercise. No need now to go down to gully, eh?

Tea
Velina Hasu Houston

Scene Four. The home of Himiko Hamilton in Junction City, Kansas, and an obscure netherworld where time moves at will. 1968.

Himiko Hamilton, a Japanese "war bride" is "a pale, delicately boned woman wearing a feminine but mysterious dress over which is a kimono of distorted colors. . . . She is beautiful, but beaten, and exudes an aura of sultry mystery. There is no lunacy in this woman, rather the sense of one who has been pushed to the edge, tried desperately to hold on, and failed." At the beginning of the play, a group of Japanese women married to American serviceman, "war brides" like Himiko, gather to clean Himiko's house following her suicide. As they discuss her life at the hands of an abusive husband and their own experiences with racism and cultural adjustment, Himiko's netherworld presence listens and interjects, unsettled and searching. In this monologue, she tells of her daughter's tragedy, the final blow that led to the decision to take her own life.

Himiko: I was born in a storm and it's never stopped raining. My only blessing is Mieko, my half-Japanese girl. I love her so much, but she was born in my storm, too. For years, I tried to talk to her, but she wasn't ready. (*A sad laugh*) Mieko is so fast, I only know what she looks like from behind. Because she's always leaving, her big Japanese *o-shiri* swaying like a flower, out looking for dreams she thinks men are going to give her. So it was a Saturday in May, Mieko wants to make me worry, so she *hitchhikes*. She's gone three days. Then the big policeman comes. "Do you have a daughter named Mieko? When's the last time you saw her, Mrs. Hamilton?" (*Breathes hard and fast; forces composure*) The last time I saw Mieko is in the dusk. She looks so Japanese, her shoulders curving like gentle hills. "Perfect kimono shoulders," her grandmother would say. (*A beat*) Mieko came home today. Someone made her dirty, stabbed her in the chest many times and then raped her as she died. Left a broom inside my little girl's body. Her brassiere was shredded by the knife. (*A beat*) There is no one for me; there never was. Even my sisters of Japan cannot bless me with sandals to cover my blistered feet as I prepare for the longest journey. (*Looks around*) Billy, is that you? Before it's too late, tell me the truth. You loved me, didn't you? Once. Once there was nobody like me. Now that I know, I can go on without you, Billy. I see you there, waiting in the mist, your strong arms ready to hold me for one last dance. But I'm going another way. Like bamboo, I sway back and forth in the wind, bending but never breaking. Never again. The war is over. Mother? Is that you? Are you waiting for me, too? (*Brief, absolute delight, addressing* MIEKO *when she was five*) Mieko-chan, I see you dancing in my best kimono: all light and laughter and . . . clean! (*The delight fades*) No, you all have to let me go now. I have a long walk ahead of me. All ties are unbound, as completely as if they never existed.

Unfinished Women Cry in No Man's Land While a Bird Dies in a Gilded Cage
Aisha Rahman

Scene 6. The Hide-A-Wee Home for Unwed Mothers. 1955.

Five young women, pregnant and unmarried, await the births of their babies on the same day Charlie Parker is dying in the boudoir of his lover. Wilma, "A Black Gal in Conflict," provokes the other girls with her sarcasm. She breaks the normal conversation about pregnancy, boyfriends, and decisions to keep or give up their babies with the news that Charlie Parker has died. In this monologue, she tells what Parker's music has meant to her and where his music lives within her.

WILMA: (*To audience.*) You know, I first dug Bird 'cause everybody was into him and used to talk about him all the time. Then when I really listened to him. . . . Dudes 'round my way would only take their special woman to dig Bird with. I went down to Birdland one night and everybody was waiting for him and when he finally showed he looked like he slept under the bandstand and hadn't shaved for weeks. I never saw anything like that and I never heard anything like his music. Charlie Parker played in tongues. . . . I don't want to give up my baby, but . . . I know that it's a boy in here. S'funny what Bird meant to me. Secretly, I always wanted to be a man 'cause they can do things and go places. Bird is the man I wanted to be. Maybe my son will be like him. Dig that. Maybe I'm giving up a Charlie Parker. Maybe I'm thinking about giving up a Charlie Parker. The baby's father? He's just someone I met at a dance. Tall, dark and good-looking. And I liked the way his smile tasted in my mouth. Anthony. He smiled at me and I smiled back and we wanted each other. He's just a man I gave myself to and I can't blame him for anything. Really. But I do because I'm here and he's. . . . (*Shrugging her shoulders helplessly.*) You know what this is? (*Puts her hands on her stomach.*) It's a curse . . . it got my mother and now it's got me . . . fatherless child, manless woman, it's deep, it's always there waiting no matter how you try to escape. I watched it pick us off like typhoid, one by one. We knew a girl had caught it when her belly got bigger and bigger and her eyes took on a certain feverish look and everybody wondered who's next . . . who's next . . . and now it's my turn. . . .

(*Music up.*)

In Anthony's room, in his bed, lying there on my back, I could feel myself far below him, I was on the bottom of an ocean and he was the moon way up over me. A moon I could smell, a moon I could touch but whose face floated in and out of my mind. His body was spread all over, covering me like space. I crouched inside of myself, listening like an animal to our silence. Then, slowly floating in through the open window, very faint at first . . . the sound of Bird's horn . . . tugging at me, taking me back to a memory I was born with. Following the music's heartbeat I took a journey I could no longer avoid and along the way I helped a woman toss her newborn baby overboard a slaveship. I joined hands with my mother as she took *her* mother's hand and I took my place in the circle of black women singing old blues. The man, spread high above me, worked over me, his sweat dripping down in my eyes and my voice screaming higher and higher along with Parker's sax . . . both sounds pouring over me, pulling me, pushing me to a point of passion, a point of pain and then . . . silence . . . and the smell of the rain falling outside as he breaks into my womb and bursts inside of me, overflowing on the sheets and bed and everything and I knew that the cycle of passion and pain, blood and birth, and aloneness had once again started, inside of me and I lay there wondering how many moons before I could become virgin again!

(*Music up as she listens for a few beats.*)

Hear that? He's not dead. Bird lives. . . . Inside here. (*Embracing her stomach.*) Bird's alive. . . . Oh yes, he's alive.

Unfinished Women Cry in No Man's Land While a Bird Dies in a Gilded Cage
Aisha Rahman

Scene 4. The Hide-A-Wee Home for Unwed Mothers. 1955.

Head Nurse Jacobs manages the young women's schedules and activities with unconcealed contempt. A middle-aged West Indian woman, highly religious and judgmental, she reflects on her personal connection to the pregnant young women.

NURSE JACOBS: (*To audience.*) I been through this day a hundred times . . . watching hundreds of girls go downstairs and make their decisions to give up their babies or . . . whatever. And I still can't . . . still can't help remembering. Yes! I had a man once. Is Gospel! He broke holes in the air with his laughter! Big-time Calypsonian. Playing from island to island. He, writing me all the time these love letters: "Darlin' . . . I lonely for you. Your heart in front of my eyes all the time. Take care of our green baby growin' inside of you, sweetheart. I missing you in that certain way." Sweet, sweet words. I getting bigger and bigger and happier and happier. I didn't have no shame *then*, only love. I getting ready the marrying things, the white dress, veil, even the eats and drinks and then . . . nothing . . . no sweet words . . . no promises . . . nothing. Nothing slowly stretches into nothing. Saviour in heaven . . . you forgive Mary Magdalene so why not me? I paid my penance for my hour of passion. I work hard . . . keep man outta my life and raise my . . . my . . . "niece." (*Angrily.*) Yes . . . Yes . . . I calling me own *daughter* my niece. You don't understand. Back home we don't have places like this. A girl in trouble has to make her own arrangements. I went to another island . . . bought myself a wedding ring and gave birth to my "niece." It's been hard . . . all these years . . . keeping my daughter a secret . . . raising up me "niece" by myself. . . . But I hanging on. . . . Praise God. . . . I hanging on!

Unmerciful Good Fortune
Edwin Sánchez

Act 2. Luz's bedroom. The Bronx.

Luz is a forty-two-year-old Puerto Rican woman who is bedridden and dying. Under the influence of heavy pain killers, she wavers between moments of lucidity, fantasy, and unbearable suffering. She is married to a Pito, seventy-seven, who first saw her in the town square in Isabela when she was twelve and he was forty-seven. Pito is devoted to the woman he describes as "My little virgin in white." Although Luz loves him, she is angry about losing her youth and longs to live. She forces her daughter Maritza, an attorney, to pretend she is "Leyda," a wild, sexual alter ego, named after Maritza's twin sister who died at birth. In this scene, Luz demands Maritza get Leyda. When Maritza wistfully asks her mother, "Where do you go when you're with Leyda?" her mother describes a life she never had.

Luz: Most of the time we go dancing. We look like sisters. We wear our colors. Hers is yellow, mine is red with mucho cleavage. We put makeup on each other and pile our hair up. Oh yeah, just so we can make it fall when we dance. Our dresses are glittery and wherever we go we make an entrance. Our walk is famous all over town. We look at everybody as we walk in and everybody, I mean everybody looks at us. Men buy us drinks and light our cigarettes. Women want to hate us, but they can't 'cause we're so beautiful. The first time we dance, we always do it together. That's after we've turned down everybody, but sweetly, you know, so they'll still ask us later. We dance with each other, Leyda and me, and the room is hypnotized. We dance with every part of us. Little by little people will come and dance next to us; trying to pretend they're dancing with us. And then we turn and face them. We dissolve in their presence. Our turns, our perfume caresses them. Our sweat pours off us and people fight to wipe our brows. Souvenirs. Proof that they danced with wild animals. I think Leyda bites them sometimes. Not hard, just hard enough to own them. And when everyone is done, when even Leyda can't dance, I'm still dancing. The band is playing just for me and I'm under the perfect white hot light. There is nobody hotter than Luz. I love you, Maritza, but this is not something you can understand. Desire is not in your vocabulary.

Weebjob
Diane Glancy

Act 2. Scene 1. The Salazar Canyon in Lincoln County, New Mexico, between Roswell and Socorro.

Suzanne Long Chalk, or Sweet Potato, is the twenty-one-year-old daughter of Gerald Long Chalk, or Weebjob, age forty-eight, a Mescalero Apache holy man. He's stern and unyielding, a little impractical, yet likable. Sweet Potato "has a mind of her own." She is unhappy with her life because she doesn't know where she belongs. She has run off several times to hitch-hike on the interstate to Gallup. Sweet Potato and Percy Willingdeer, or Pick Up, Weebjob's forty-three-year-old best friend, have fallen in love, much to the disapproval of her father. Pick Up has brought Sweet Potato back to her father's house after finding her on the highway once again. In this monologue, she tells him why she runs away.

SWEET POTATO: When I'm standing on the road with my thumb up, the heat trying to take my breath, the fear of passing cars pounding in my chest, I feel one with the land. The shrubs speak to me like children. The dry river beds maybe without a trickle of water. I wash in the heat and feel alive on Interstate 40 West. Not straining for existence any longer, but filled with meaning. I forget I'm a reject of this world. When I'm on my way to Gallup, I'm INDIAN. I like these worn hills with wrinkles like an old man's face, and with sand as brown as our skin. The divided highway is not like 380 through the canyon. Wind plays with my hair and the heat laughs. . . . The terrible heat that pulls one into itself, and windows of the skin are open and we are running with the heat. Not hardly anyone knows but us. I like the morning sun on my back and the long fingers of the evening shadow across the highway. I want to go again across the Cibolo County line to Gallup. . . . Palomino rocks. Mountains and plateaus. Sometimes I sit in the shade of a bush and listen to the cars pass. I don't ride with anyone who stops. I look them over first. There are white men who would use me. . . . That's why they can't see and feel the life of the desert, and can't hear the Great Spirit walking in the heat—in the midst of the fiery furnace. When I get as far as Mesita I know I'll make it. Rock slides where the highway cuts through the plateaus. Payute. Cubero. James goes up into the Pinos Mountains, but I have to go farther.

Wines in the Wilderness
Alice Childress

Harlem, New York. Bill's apartment. The summer of 1964. The morning after a riot.

Tommy is "a woman factory worker aged thirty" who has been brought to the studio of Bill Jameson, a thirty-three-year-old painter, by two of his friends who think she would make a perfect model for his current project. Bill is painting a triptych entitled "'Wine in the Wilderness' . . . Three canvases on black womanhood. . . ." The first represents innocence and is called "Black Girlhood." The second is "Mother Africa, regal black womanhood in her noblest form." When he meets Tommy, Bill thinks she's perfect for the third painting, "the kinda chick that is grass roots . . . no, not grass roots. . . . I mean she's underneath the grass roots. The lost woman . . . what the society has made of our women. . . . She's ignorant, unfeminine, coarse, rude . . . vulgar . . . a poor, dumb chick that's had her behind kicked until she's numb. . . ."

Tommy doesn't understand why Bill wants to paint her; suspiciously she cooperates. During the sitting she loses her patience with his condescending and judgmental ways; eventually she disarms him, revealing that she is the true "Wine in the Wilderness." They recognize a common spirit and begin to fall in love. The next morning, when Bill's friends arrive, Tommy inadvertently discovers the real reason why Bill wanted to paint her and what she symbolized to him. She confronts them all for deceiving her and decides to go back to her own crowd.

Tommy: I don't stay mad; it's here today and gone tomorrow. I'm sorry your feelin's got hurt, . . . but when I'm hurt I turn and hurt back. Somewhere, in the middle of last night, I thought the old me was gone, . . . lost forever, and gladly. But today was flippin' time, so back I flipped. Now it's "turn the other cheek" time. If I can go through life other-cheekin' the white folk, . . . guess y'all can be other-cheeked too. But I'm going back to the nitty-gritty crowd, where the talk is we-ness and us-ness. I hate to do it but I have to thank you 'cause I'm walkin' out with much more than I brought in. (*Goes over and looks at the queen in the "Wine in the Wilderness" painting.*) Tomorrow-Marie had such a lovely yesterday.

(BILL *takes her hand; she gently removes it from his grasp.*)

Tommy: Bill, I don't have to wait for anybody's by-your-leave to be a "Wine in the Wilderness" woman. I can be it if I wanta, . . . and I am. I am. I am. I'm not the one you made up and painted, the very pretty lady who can't talk back, . . . but I'm "Wine in the Wilderness.". . . alive and kickin', me . . . Tomorrow-Marie, cussin' and fightin' and lookin' out for my damn self 'cause ain' nobody else 'round to do it, dontcha know. And, Cynthia, if my hair is straight, or if it's natural, or if I wear a wig, or take it off, . . . that's all right; because wigs . . . shoes . . . hats . . . bags . . . and even this. . . . (*She picks up the African throw she wore a few moments before . . . fingers it.*) They're just what . . . what you call . . . access . . . (*Fishing for the word.*) . . . like what you wear with your Easter outfit . . .

(CYNTHIA: *Accessories.*)

Tommy: Thank you my sister. Accessories. Somethin' you add on or take off. The real thing is takin' place on the inside . . . that's where the action is. That's "Wine in the Wilderness,". . . a woman that's a real one and a good one. And y'all just better believe I'm it. (*She proceeds to the door.*)

Acknowledgments

The editor wishes to acknowledge and thank New WORLD Theater staff: **Brandon Anderson**, **Lucy Mae**, **San Pablo Burns**, **Jesus MacLean**, **Joe Salvatore**, **Jessica Shadoian**, **Susanne Mussmann**, **Angel Hardy** and **Jen Werner** for assistance with research and **Dennis Conway**, **Yvonne Mendez**, **Lisa Hori-Garcia**, **Karima Robinson**, **Mary Muratore**, and **Javiera Benavente** for keeping the theater going strong during this project. Special thanks to **Fred Tillis** and **Lee Edwards** for their mentorship, and to **Len Berkman**, **Shelby Jiggetts-Tivony**, **Richard Trousdell**, **Harley Erdman**, and **Betsy Theobald** for their sound advice. For their love, patience and support, thank-you to my children and husband: **Chinua Akimaro Thelwell**, **Mikiko Akemi Thelwell**, and **Andrew Condron**.

Permissions and Play Sources

138